What people are saying about *Major Gift Fundraising for Small Shops*

Amy Eisenstein takes the complex subject of major gift fundraising and distills it down to its essential elements. The book provides a clear, methodical approach that any organization can follow. Great tips, real-world stories, checklists, sample forms, and more make this a book that you will keep on your desk and refer to often—if you want to raise more money ~~than you ever~~ have thought possible.

Michael J. Rosen, CFRE
Author, *Donor-Centered Planned Gift Marketing*
President, ML Innovations

This book is a must-read for those just getting their feet wet in nonprofit fundraising as well as for those looking to build a major gifts program with limited resources. While taking minimal time in an already-packed schedule, Amy Eisenstein breaks down major gift fundraising into bite-sized pieces with her insightful approach that builds upon itself to create a successful program. Her refreshing writing style walks you through the intimidating process of fundraising with clarity and purpose.

Linda Henderson
Director, Pawnee Valley Community Hospital Foundation

Two thumbs up for Amy Eisenstein's book on major gifts for small shops. The key question readers of fundraising books must ask themselves is: "Will this book help me raise more money?" I guarantee that if you follow the advice in this book, you will raise much more money for your cause.

Harvey McKinnon
Author, *The 11 Questions Every Donor Asks*
Coauthor, *The Power of Giving: How Giving Back Enriches Us All*
(number-one best seller)

A clearly written, step-by-step guide to successfully cultivating, raising, and closing major gifts. Amy Eisenstein's book is an indispensable read for all fundraisers who are considering major gifts for their organization.

Celia Hagerman
Major Gifts Associate, American Red Cross, Florida West Coast Region

Think your organization's too small to raise major gifts? Well, think again! Major gift fundraising is even more important for you. Read this remarkable little book and springboard your organization into the future!

Andrea Kihlstedt
Capital Campaign Magic

This is the fundraising blueprint you've been looking for! Amy Eisenstein provides a clear, ambitious, but realistic path to building a productive fundraising program for your small organization—or to taking your fundraising to the next level. Jump on it.

Nancy Schwartz
Blogger/Speaker/Consultant, GettingAttention.org

*In **Major Gifts Fundraising for Small Shops**, Amy Eisenstein makes good on the promise of her book's title. With deep empathy for small-shop fundraisers, she covers every base, yet the material is never overwhelming. She addresses the issues that are likely to hold us back in a no-nonsense yet positive tone: "Yes, you **can** do this, and you can even have **fun** doing it!" This book left me feeling reassured, energized, and motivated.*
Brenda Hebert
Director of Development, CASA for Children of Essex County

Amy Eistenstein digs deep into all the important questions you need to address to start building a major gift program. A great tool for anyone who is hesitant to jump in. (You should!)
Brian Saber
President, Asking Matters

*It's quite a promise: that even a small organization can create a pipeline of major gifts— devoting just five hours a week to the effort. Of course, you **will** have to read Amy Eisenstein's nuts-and-bolts book first. But once that's done and you've digested chapters like "Creating an Army of Advocates and the Role of Social Media," you'll be ready to proceed with confidence, thanks to this first-of-its-kind, super-solid, step-by-step guide. Five hours a week gets your organization in line for those juicy $5,000 and higher gifts that put big roses in NGO cheeks.*
Tom Ahern
Author, *Seeing Through a Donor's Eyes*

Amy Eistenstein knows what it takes to bring in major gifts and shows small shops how to replicate that success in this book. If you want to raise major gifts, you should read this book!
Dan Blakemore
Assistant Director of Development, International House

It's way past time to raise major gifts as part of your annual fundraising. I've been promoting this for years. Finally, here is the step-by-step guide to do it. Amy Eisenstein's book explains why—and then provides step-by-step details for you and your boss and your board. Do it—with this guide at your side.
Simone P. Joyaux, ACFRE
Author, *Firing Lousy Board Members, Keep Your Donors,*
and *Strategic Fund Development*

Major Gift Fundraising for Small Shops *has given me the tools to raise major donations in as few as five hours a week! This must-read book is for anyone wanting to make a significant improvement in their organization. Amy Eisenstein outlines strategies to increase your donations and strengthen your donor relationships.*
Stacie Cook
Executive Director, Madelia Community Hospital Foundation

Major Gift Fundraising
for Small Shops

How to Leverage Your Annual Fund in Only Five Hours per Week

Amy Eisenstein, MPA, ACFRE

*Charity*Channel ®
PRESS ™

Major Gift Fundraising for Small Shops:
How to Leverage Your Annual Fund in Only Five Hours per Week

One of the **In the Trenches**™ series

Published by
CharityChannel Press, an imprint of CharityChannel LLC
30021 Tomas, Suite 300
Rancho Santa Margarita, CA 92688-2128 USA

CharityChannel.com

ISBN Print Book: 978-1-938077-56-2 | ISBN eBook: 978-1-938077-57-9

Library of Congress Control Number: 2014933614

13 12 11 10 9 8 7 6 5 4 3 2 1

Printed in the United States of America

This and most CharityChannel Press books are available at special quantity discounts for bulk purchases for sales promotions, premiums, fundraising, or educational use. For information, contact CharityChannel Press, 30021 Tomas, Suite 300, Rancho Santa Margarita, CA 92688-2128 USA. +1 949-589-5938

Publisher's Acknowledgments

This book was produced by a team dedicated to excellence; please send your feedback to editors@charitychannel.com.

We first wish to acknowledge the tens of thousands of peers who call charitychannel.com their online professional home. Your enthusiastic support for the **In the Trenches**™ series is the wind in our sails.

Members of the team who produced this book include:

Editors

Acquisitions Editor: Stephen Nill

Comprehensive Editor: Stephen Nill

Copy Editor: Jill McLain

Production

In the Trenches Series Design: Deborah Perdue

Layout Editor: Jill McLain

Administrative

CharityChannel LLC: Stephen Nill, CEO

Marketing and Public Relations: John Millen and Linda Lysakowski

About the Author

Amy Eisenstein, MPA, CFRE, ACFRE, is also the author of *Raising More with Less: An Essential Fundraising Guide for Nonprofit Professionals and Board Members* and of *50 A$ks in 50 Weeks: A Guide to Better Fundraising for Your Small Development Shop* as well as a contributing author to *You and Your Nonprofit: Practical Advice and Tips from the CharityChannel Professional Community*. Through writing, speaking, and consulting, Amy helps nonprofit staff and board members raise more money for the organizations they love.

Amy is the principal and owner of Tri Point Fundraising, a full-service consulting firm that supports nonprofit organizations with executive and development coaching, capital and annual campaign consulting, development planning, individual and major gifts programs, and board and staff member training and development. She is also a frequent speaker at conferences and a facilitator of board and staff retreats.

Amy received a master's degree in public administration and nonprofit management from Wagner Graduate School at New York University and a bachelor's degree from Douglass College at Rutgers University. She currently serves as the president of the board of the Association of Fundraising Professionals–New Jersey Chapter. She became an ACFRE in 2013, has been a Certified Fundraising Executive (CFRE) since 2004, and became a certified Master Trainer in 2009.

You can reach Amy through her website at tripointfundraising.com. She would love to hear from you about your successes and challenges with raising major gifts! Please contact her at amy@tripointfundraising.com.

Dedication

This book is dedicated to all the nonprofit staff and board members who are working hard to make the world a better place.

Author's Acknowledgments

As with any book, this one would not have been possible without the love, support, and contributions of many people. I would like to begin by thanking my wonderful friend, colleague, editor, and publisher, Stephen C. Nill, CEO of CharityChannel Press, whom I have had the pleasure of working with and getting to know over the last few years.

Many thanks to Dawn Wolfe. There are no words to thank you for your contributions. This book would not have been possible without your help and support.

And last but not least, to my loving husband and children, Alan, Ethan, and Zoe, who have been only mildly neglected throughout the writing process, but who received a puppy this year to alleviate some of my working-mommy guilt!

Contents

Summary of Chapters

The Secret to Successful Fundraising: Creating a Culture of Philanthropy and Professionalism at Your Organization. Chapter One provides you with an explanation of a culture of philanthropy and of how to recruit and retain effective board members who will be fantastic fundraising "force multipliers."

Creating Your Strategy. In Chapter Two, we will cover the difference between annual and capital campaigns, why it's important to grow and mature as an organization, and how major gifts will help you with this important development.

The Secret Weapon of Major Gifts: Engaging Your Board. Chapter Three provides a further discussion of the board's role in major gifts and other fundraising. I discuss the importance of proper recruitment, training, and support to hold members accountable and make them more comfortable with fundraising, as well as how to plan and execute effective retreats and regular meetings to keep your board engaged, passionate, and ready and willing to raise money.

The Role of Social Media. In Chapter Four, we take a look at the increasing role of social media in raising awareness and funds, including major gifts. I discuss how to get involved in social media today to reach your donors of tomorrow.

What Does Bulk Mail Have to Do with Major Gifts? In Chapter Five, you will learn why bulk mail is a valuable tool for identifying potential major gift prospects. We also discuss why it's still worthwhile to use postal mail.

Who Will You Ask for Major Gifts? Chapter Six covers how to use your database to identify prospective major donors. It also provides specific instructions for finalizing your list of top twenty prospects.

Researching Your Prospects: The Fine Line between Professional and Creepy. Chapter Seven discusses the ethics of donor/prospect research and what you need to know about your major gift prospects. It also covers how and why to protect your donors' privacy, the basics of Internet research, and the best research tool of all: asking.

The Art and Science of Getting a Meeting: How to Meet with People You Know—and with People You Don't. In Chapter Eight, I discuss the goal of your first meeting. It may not be what you think. It includes a discussion of who to bring, where to meet, how to get the meeting in the first place, what to say while you're there, and how to make sure you have a follow-up plan that will bring you closer to asking for a major gift.

How to Build Deeper Relationships with Major Gift Prospects. In Chapter Nine, you will learn about cultivation, the fine art of building close relationships with the people you'll be asking for major gifts. We cover the steps involved in the cultivation process and the importance of individualizing your cultivation plan for each prospect.

Get Ready to Ask. In Chapter Ten, you will learn when the right time is to ask for a major gift and who should attend your ask meeting and why. We'll also discuss how to determine how much to ask for.

The Moment of Truth (Time to Ask). Finally, in Chapter Eleven is about the Ask! We'll cover what to bring to the ask meeting and a sample meeting agenda. I discuss the importance of knowing when to be quiet after you've asked as well as preparing for *yes, no,* and *maybe.*

More Than Simply *Thank You.* In Chapter Twelve, you'll learn about the importance of thanking donors and letting them know how their gifts have been used. I discuss the "Rule of Seven Thank-Yous," why you should have a board member call to thank donors, and the many ways to thank your donors.

Considering a Capital Campaign? In Chapter Thirteen, you will learn the differences between annual fund and capital campaigns. If you're even considering a capital campaign, read this chapter to discover how to know if your organization is ready to launch a capital campaign.

Can a Small Shop Really Do Planned Giving? In Chapter Fourteen, you will learn all about planned giving and what steps your organization needs to take to safely accept planned gifts.

Moving on Up: Taking Your Organization to the Next Level. Chapter Fifteen covers moving your organization to the next stage in its development, which includes the importance of donor retention, as well as becoming a fundraising superstar through professional development.

Foreword

In his famous speech, "Acres of Diamonds," Russell Conwell tells the tale of an African farmer who sells his land and travels the continent in pursuit of diamonds. The man's search is in vain, and he eventually dies a poor and discontented soul. A rich diamond mine, it turns out, was there on the land the farmer had sold. The moral of the story is, of course, that most people look everywhere for opportunity, success, and happiness—except the one place where they're most likely to find it: under their own two feet.

It's been my experience, too, that most nonprofit organizations fail to fully mine the diamonds hidden within their own databases. Instead, they're continuously looking for new donors and are in endless pursuit of the next big trend in fundraising.

So how can you find your "Acres of Diamonds" within your own agency?

Within the pages of this book, in only five hours a week, Amy Eisenstein will guide you safely and surely through the challenges of getting your organization ready for major gift fundraising, all the way up to that all-important ask—*and beyond.*

If you've been in fundraising for any length of time, you've no doubt heard of the "90/10 Rule." In its simplest terms, it means that 90 percent of the funding comes from 10 percent of our donors. Yet far too often, the majority of our time is spent focused on low-yield fundraising activities, such as events. Amy argues that the key to successful long-term, sustainable fundraising lies in dramatically increasing your fundraising income from individual donors. And savvy fundraisers will do well to heed her advice.

But how can you get started? With Amy at the helm, guiding you in developing your organization's major gifts program, you'll find it's absolutely doable. Amy doesn't pull any punches. She makes it clear, if you're going to succeed in major gifts, that everyone will need to be on board and that effective and consistent fundraising training is a must. It's a commitment. Throughout the book, she explains key fundraising concepts, the difference between major gifts and capital campaigns, how to determine exactly what constitutes a major gift for *your* organization, the importance of gift acceptance policies, job responsibilities for your major gift team, the role of online fundraising in major gifts fundraising, the role of direct mail, maintaining your database, and more.

In short, she cuts to the chase to show you that major gift fundraising is something that, yes, you can do. It just takes focus and Amy's know-how, marvelously outlined within these pages.

I first met Amy at an Association of Grant Professionals conference where we were both presenting and have gotten to know her well in the ensuing years. I love her warmly reassuring, solid, can-do approach to tackling the challenges of "small shop" fundraising. **You will too.**

Pamela Grow
Publisher of *The Grow Report*, a weekly enews created for small shop fundraisers
Founder of *Simple Development Systems*, online fundraising training for nonprofit
    executive directors, development directors, and board members
PamelaGrow.com

Introduction

Do you spend most of your time spinning on the "hamster wheel" of fundraising? In other words, with grant writing and event planning? Do you want to raise more but don't feel as though you have the time or know-how to make it happen?

Believe me, after working with dozens of small fundraising shops like yours, I get it. But here's something you need to know: You will never be able to help your organization make the leap from a good to a great nonprofit by relying on grants, events, and small donors alone.

However, you *can* do something about it. You can transform your organization and vastly increase your ability to raise funds, and you can do it in just five hours per week!

I began thinking about how to get smaller nonprofits to have success in the arena of major gifts several years ago. The result was something I called the "Major Gifts Challenge."

Just what *is* the Major Gifts Challenge?

In January of 2013, I set out to create a program on my blog to allow even small nonprofit fundraising shops to start benefitting from the kind of income that can really come only from major gifts. The challenge took readers through the entire process of identifying, researching, stewarding, and asking prospects for major gifts.

The results were fantastic! Nonprofit professionals who had never considered major gifts started putting their toes in the water and discovered something I learned many years ago—that major gift fundraising is far more efficient, and far less time- and work-intensive, than either special events or writing and administering grants.

If you look at those blog posts, though, you'll notice one major change between the online Major Gifts Challenge and this book: The online version called for only two hours a week while this more complete book version requires you to set aside five hours. Why? For one thing, my readers and I discovered that two hours a week wasn't quite enough. However, two hours *was* enough to get them started—to dip their toes into major gift fundraising and to start having some success.

Can I really become a successful at raising major gifts in only five hours a week?

Yes! You can raise major gifts in only five hours per week, but you must commit five hours a week, every week, to make it happen! When people fail to raise major gifts, it's because they think about it, and stress about it, more than they actually do it! That's what the Major Gifts Challenge on my blog, and this book, is all about.

Also, see the **Appendix**, "Finding Five Hours per Week," with its sample calendars to help you schedule your time.

important

Since you've picked up this book, I know you're ready to do more than start. You want to see big results, and that's going to take some time. That's the most important reason I've expanded the challenge from two hours a week to five: It's time for your nonprofit to realize even more success with major gifts!

"Five hours a week!" I hear you saying. "Where can I fit another five hours a week into everything we're already doing? We have three events to plan, another grant coming up, and then there's our mailing to consider… We just don't have five hours to give unless we cut something else."

And I have to be honest with you. Creating a successful major gifts program may mean you'll need to streamline the efforts you put into other areas.

Imagine that you've put just five hours a week toward working on major gifts. You identified your twenty prospects, researched them, and cultivated them. And after approximately twelve months, you started receiving four- or perhaps even five-figure gifts. In approximately 12 percent of your work time, you've just increased your organization's operating budget by as much as you would raise at a special event or possibly even your year-end mailing! And by concentrating on just twenty donors, you've spent *much, much* less money than you do on events or mail campaigns.

Let's take a look at the numbers. For our argument's sake, let's assume that your organization receives $100,000 in grant dollars and that you spend about 50 percent of your total work time writing grants. If you spend five hours on major gifts (approximately 12 percent of your total work time, assuming you work forty hours) and receive ten gifts totaling $50,000, your time has certainly been well spent!

In my experience, the best way to get from where you are to where you want to be, fundraising-wise, is to increase your annual fund and to drastically increase fundraising income from individual donors through major gifts.

Why? Here's another fundraising rule: On average, 80 percent of your donations will come from 20 percent of your donors. The other 80 percent of your donors will give only 20 percent of your total dollars raised. Not convinced? Take a look at your top 20 percent of donors and total their giving.

Given this rule, where would you rather spend your time? Maximizing the amount of funding given by your top 20 percent of donors? Or on that "hamster wheel" chasing after the other 80 percent?

However, I want to make it clear that I'm not suggesting that you stop looking for grants, sending postal and electronic mailings, or holding events!

Until you and your donors are accustomed to asking for and giving major gifts it's important to maintain your other "tried and true" methods of fundraising during the other thirty-five (or more) hours per week you spend on fundraising. As you start to achieve success in the major gifts arena, I am confident you will dedicate more and more time to raising major gifts as you start to see bigger and better results. Once you do, you will be able to hire additional staff members to help with direct mail, events, and grant fundraising, which are also critical to any comprehensive fundraising program.

I believe that every nonprofit organization should have a diversified fundraising plan that includes a variety of strategies and efforts. This means having multiple streams of revenue from multiple sources including grants, events, bulk mail, and online. However, most nonprofit fundraising professionals and volunteers are the weakest in their individual giving skills and experience. That's the reason I've written this book—to provide you with the skills and experience you need to truly transform your fundraising program and your organization as a whole, because you can't have a truly diversified fundraising program without including major gifts.

Why? Because individual major gifts are the largest source of potential donations for your organization. According to Giving USA's annual report, approximately 80 percent of donations in the United States are given by individuals—not corporations or foundations. I can almost hear you thinking, "Yes, but aren't the vast majority of those donations in the form of smaller gifts?" You're right. They are. But, again, the point of this book isn't to show you how to go after that vast majority. Instead, you'll be spending your valuable time on the top 20 percent of them. (Of course, if some of your major gift efforts *also* result in an increase in smaller gifts, I think we can agree that would be a wonderful side effect!)

The facts about individual giving show that if your fundraising shop isn't cultivating the potential major donors in your community, you are literally leaving money on the table— money your organization could use to change lives and save lives.

However, while major gift solicitation is the least expensive fundraising method (not including planned giving), the fact is that there is both an art and a science to creating a successful major gift program. And it takes time and effort!

As part of that effort, we need to overcome the fact that too many people are uncomfortable about asking for gifts! Therefore, this book teaches executive directors, development professionals, and board members everything they need to know about donor identification, cultivation, stewardship, and the all-important ask. It doesn't assume that you have access to sophisticated research or even donor screening programs. It *does* focus on your ability to significantly increase your organization's annual revenue—*without any additional resources*—by incorporating individual, face-to-face asks as part of your ongoing annual fund program.

In order to create your own successful major gifts program all you need is this book, five hours a week, and the commitment to keep at it until you succeed.

Why Not Start with a Capital Campaign?

This book is *not* about capital campaigns. Why? Because most organizations try to make the leap into the world of capital campaigns without first increasing their annual funds or learning the basics of individual giving. That's like trying to run a marathon before learning how to walk, as one of my current clients is learning the hard way. This client, a school, jumped into its first capital campaign without first having any experience in individual giving. Now I'm working to give the staff and board a crash course in the midst of this important campaign—certainly not the best time to be practicing fundraising skills and techniques!

In addition, this book isn't about capital campaigns because, in order to increase your chances of being truly successful with such an effort, you first need to have built solid relationships with your major prospects and donors—and the confidence to ask each of them for a gift that's ten times (or more) the size of what they usually give!

Finally, this book doesn't talk about capital campaigns because I want you to start seeing success in a year or less and to be able to use the funds for your current programs and services. Once you grow your program by increasing your annual fund with major gifts, you will be in a much better position to consider launching a capital campaign.

Get Ready, Get Set, Get Major Gifts!

Before you start soliciting major gifts from individuals, you need to be able to articulate why your organization exists. What are your mission and vision? Who does your organization exist to serve? Why does your organization matter in this world? What difference do you make? You need to be able to answer those questions articulately and with passion.

You also need to find individuals who are philanthropic and have money to give. However, this isn't always as difficult as it may sound! Your donors don't necessarily need to be "rich." Many working and middle-class people can, and do, make very generous donations to the organizations they care deeply about. From now on, it is your mission to find these people, cultivate them, and ask them for money!

But how much should you ask for? Years of experience have taught me that one of the biggest mistakes that executive directors and fundraising professionals make is not asking for enough. That's why one of the first things this book addresses is how to determine what constitutes a major gift for your organization.

Learning to Love Fundraising

It's possible that before you start to learn how to ask for major gifts you'll need to overcome some fears. Fundraising is often perceived as scary by those who haven't done it. However, once you get started and have a few successes under your belt, you may even come to enjoy it.

How could you possibly come to enjoy asking for money? For one thing—believe it or not—more often than not, the donor will thank *you*! Why? Because, by providing the opportunity to give, you've helped your donor make a real difference in your community, and making a difference feels great! Think about the last time you made a gift to charity. Didn't you feel wonderful?

Major gift fundraising isn't about "twisting arms" or shaking cans. It's about finding people who share your organization's passion and inviting them to become part of the solution to the problems you're addressing.

Fundraising is like an important puzzle, one that board and staff members need to work together to solve. It's up to all of you to identify and inspire others to give to your organization. I hope you will share this book with your executive director, your fundraising team, and your board members. They all need to be involved with fundraising if you're going to catapult your organization to the next level and beyond.

Please feel free to contact me if you have any additional questions or concerns after reading the book, and let me know how it goes. I can't wait to hear from you!

Best wishes for your fundraising success.

Part One

You *Can* Raise Major Gifts in Only Five Hours per Week!

Part One sets the stage to make sure you are prepared to raise major gifts. It focuses on what needs to happen before you can raise major gifts in terms of board and staff roles and responsibilities as well as other types of fundraising and infrastructure that must be in place. You want to have a culture of philanthropy at your organization—or at least be working to create one—as well as fully understand and be able to articulate the reason you need to raise major gifts, which is part of your strategy. Part One also covers the importance of a social media presence and the role of bulk mail in major gifts. This part lays the foundation for raising major gifts.

Chapter One

The Secret to Successful Fundraising: Creating a Culture of Philanthropy and Professionalism at Your Organization

IN THIS CHAPTER

···→ How and why to create a culture of philanthropy

···→ The importance of properly recruiting and training board members

···→ Why your staff needs ongoing training

···→ How to keep the passion for your mission alive

Given the title of this chapter, you can assume that I believe some of the key secrets to successful fundraising are (1) having a culture of philanthropy, and (2) creating a professional work environment at your organization. These two key ingredients are lead indicators as to whether or not you will be successful at major gifts fundraising. The first, a culture of philanthropy, refers to how board and staff members act with regard to giving, raising money, generosity, and gratitude. The second, having a professional work environment, refers to mutual respect between staff and board members as well as the understanding that staff needs a professional work environment, support from their colleagues, and continuing education to do their job.

What Is a Culture of Philanthropy?

In organizations with a culture of philanthropy, everyone—from the janitor to the CEO and from the board to all the other volunteers—deeply understands that philanthropy is the key to accomplishing their mission. Philanthropy pays the bills and the salaries. It funds the programs, and it is a powerful, positive force for making communities better places to live.

A culture of philanthropy translates into specific actions:

◆ Each staff member understands that every person they come into contact with is a potential supporter—and they act accordingly.

◆ Proper donor stewardship, i.e., thanking donors for their gifts, is just one aspect of creating a culture of philanthropy. In addition, that "attitude of gratitude" needs to permeate everything from your organization's written messaging to the way staff people answer the phone.

◆ In organizations with a culture of philanthropy, each member of the board of directors plays an important role in major gift fundraising *and* makes at least one major gift every year. Not only that, but frequently each staff member also gives something back to the organization, even if it's just a token amount.

◆ Finally, organizations with a culture of philanthropy recognize that there are many ways to give and show appreciation. From the senior citizen who spends ten hours a week stuffing envelopes to the donor who makes a five-figure gift. (And you never know. Those senior citizens may end up making major gifts in their wills!)

Sadly, though, not all nonprofit professionals understand that, ultimately, everyone involved in the organization is an important member of the fundraising team—particularly when it comes to raising major gifts. Sometimes executive directors tell me, "I just hired my first development director, so I don't have to do the fundraising anymore."

Wrong! The opposite is actually true: The more people involved with fundraising at your organization, the more money you will raise.

This seems obvious *because it is true*.

However, most organizations don't work that way. Instead, the fundraising at too many organizations falls primarily to a single person: the executive director or the development director.

Creating a Culture of Philanthropy: Theory and Best Practice

You may know conceptually that the executive director and board members are supposed to be involved in fundraising (particularly major gift fundraising) but not know exactly what they should be doing. They may not be sure of what's expected of them either.

So…

Let's discuss theory and best practice, and then get to reality.

Fortunately, theory and best practice are more or less the same: Each member of the team has a specific role. And when all the players perform their roles well, fundraising is often easy and successful.

The Executive Director

The executive director is the organization's visionary and chief relationship builder. Donors want to meet the CEO because the person in charge (the CEO or executive director) has the power to set the vision and oversee the implementation of programs. If the executive director's vision matches the vision of donors, then donors can feel confident that their funding will be used as they desire.

Board Members

Your organization's board of directors is the "force multiplier" for your organization. What does that mean? If you're an executive director, you're no doubt painfully aware that you can't be at every meeting or event where your organization should be represented. Nor do you have the time or the energy to find, meet, and cultivate everyone in your community who shares a passion for your organization's mission. This is where the members of your board come in. The best board members are well-regarded—and well-connected—members of your community. These people are your organization's ambassadors. By giving of their time and money, they demonstrate in a public way that yours is a vital organization deserving of the community's support. Successful fundraising is about building relationships based on trust, and your board exists, in large part, to bring and build those relationships. Add an effective, development-minded board of directors to an effective, development-minded executive director, and you'll find yourself with a major gifts campaign that is several times as effective as it would otherwise be.

Development Director

In theory and best practice, the development director is part choreographer, part member of the troupe. It's the development director's job to research prospects, set up donor meetings (and occasionally attend such meetings), guide the stewardship process, and provide fundraising training and support to the board and executive director alike. Ideally, the development director becomes familiar enough with your organization's top donors to be able to "match-make" between donors and board members with whom they are most likely to hit it off. Unlike the executive director, the development director's role is more "behind the scenes" and preparing board members and the executive director to meet with donors.

The Reality

Sadly, though, what frequently happens is that the development director alone is expected

> Each member of the fundraising "team" has an important role to play:
>
> ◆ The executive director is the visionary and the public "face" of the organization.
>
> ◆ The board members bring credibility and relationships.
>
> ◆ The development director helps coordinate all the moving parts.
>
> One person cannot and should not be expected to play all the distinct roles.

important

to fill not just the role of development director but the board's and executive director's roles as well—and very little gets accomplished when one person tries to fill so many different roles at once.

Do you want to be truly successful with major gifts fundraising? If so, it's time to engage your board members (if you haven't already done so) by creating a culture of philanthropy at your organization.

How can you change the attitudes and actions of your board (and/or) executive director? The answer lies in proper recruitment and ongoing training, which will be discussed shortly.

Why Do People Give?

Before we discuss specific ways to create a culture change at your organization, it's important to think about the reasons people give to nonprofits.

Think about a time you've given to a charity. Why did you make the gift? Did a friend ask you? Did you get a request in the mail or by email? What was your relationship with that organization?

Before going out to raise more money, you need to ask yourself why someone would give to your organization.

Would you make a gift to your organization? *Have* you? This year?

If not, what's stopping you? Whether you're staff or a volunteer, it's much easier to ask someone else for money once you've made a gift yourself. When you donate, you have skin in the game and can speak more genuinely.

People give for a variety of reasons. The number-one reason is because they're asked. People rarely give when they're not asked, so asking is key!

Other reasons people give:

The number-one reason people give is because they're asked.

important

◆ They care about a cause
   or organization.

◆ They are asked by someone
   they know.

◆ They feel guilt—or a sense of obligation.

Clearly, people feel the best about giving when they feel that their donations will make a difference in the world. They are doing their part; they've made a contribution. Most importantly, when you make people feel good about giving to your organization, they are much more likely to give again and again, and to give increasingly higher amounts.

It's up to you as a professional or volunteer fundraiser to tap into that "feel good" part of the brain so that people want to give to your organization.

Recruiting Board Members Correctly from the Start

A huge part of successfully creating a culture of philanthropy at your organization depends on having effective board members—board members who are willing and able to fill their roles as advocates and community leaders. Recruiting and retaining such board members is also a key secret to successful major gifts fundraising.

As you probably know from experience, it's much harder to turn (convert) "bad" (ineffective) board members into great ones, so it's better to start with good ones in the first place. You can avoid recruiting ineffective board members in the future by creating a board recruitment system that ensures new members know their roles and responsibilities from the start.

The first step in recruiting effective board members is creating a written job description that clearly lays out the roles and responsibilities that are expected of members of your board. These responsibilities should include both helping with fundraising and making a personal financial contribution.

Many organizations I've worked with feel so desperate to get "bodies" on the board that they're willing to take "anyone"—and then wonder why those individuals won't help with fundraising or make gifts themselves.

Don't let this happen to you! I'll discuss this in greater detail in **Chapter Seven**, but it has to be mentioned here as well, because this is one of the keys to fundraising success.

Training Your Board

The most successful major gifts campaigns that I have ever been a part of or witnessed have all enjoyed significant levels of board engagement. You can't achieve this via great recruitment alone. The next step is training and support.

I was once hired to consult with a nonprofit preschool for inner-city children. One of this organization's most obvious issues was with its board. The board members weren't making donations. So, of course, I asked if prospective board members were advised during the recruitment process that donating would be one of their responsibilities should they join.

Can you guess the answer? That's right. They hadn't established a culture of philanthropy, one where board members understand their responsibility to give. In fact, the opposite was true. They had assured the incoming board members that they *wouldn't* need to make donations in order to serve on the board.

No wonder the board wasn't making donations!

If you want your board members to actively participate in the fundraising process, you need to provide them with ongoing training and support, both at annual board retreats and at every board meeting.

Training Professional Staff

I'm currently working for an inner-city, after-school youth choir. Although music is the organization's central mission, it provides so much more: help with homework, nutritious after-school snacks, a summer camp, etc. The young people who graduate from this organization enjoy a 100 percent college attendance rate!

However, like so many other small nonprofits, this organization began as a grassroots effort in the basement of a church staffed by well-meaning volunteers. Now that they've achieved such amazing results, it's time for them to put on their rocket shoes and fly to the next stage of their development.

And that's exactly what they're doing! They've put together an ambitious strategic plan that includes significant programmatic growth—which in turn calls for significant fundraising. They're received funding for capacity building. Among other things, they've used those funds to hire me to train their board—not just at an annual retreat but at every board meeting for the next two years!

While not every organization is going to have the means (at first) to invest in this level of professional training, the fact remains that every nonprofit needs to invest as much as possible to in order to realize the most fundraising success.

stories from the real world

Training isn't only for board members. It's important that members of the development staff and your executive director receive ongoing, formal fundraising training as well.

The vast majority of professional fundraisers and executive directors have little or no formal fundraising training. Why? Because, until recently, there haven't been many formal educational programs on fundraising. Today, colleges and universities are starting to add fundraising as an undergraduate major and even as a master's program, but not many current staff have the time and/or resources to obtain a second or third degree.

Formal, ongoing training in the field is essential because while some aspects of fundraising are intuitive, many are not. And best practices on fundraising are developing every day. The things that were true yesterday about direct mail, and especially about online fundraising, aren't necessarily true today.

A small investment in fundraising training can yield big results. Make room in your budget for your development director and executive director to attend at least one fundraising conference and a few local training opportunities every year. Doing so is a wise investment that will pay off in an invigorated staff with new ideas!

Passion and Storytelling

How do you keep your staff and board members passionate about what you do? After all, if they're not excited by your cause, why should anyone else be?

The secret to creating and maintaining the passion is to develop good stories that highlight the importance of your organization. I also encourage you to incorporate a "mission moment" into all your board meetings.

This can be done in a variety of ways:

- ◆ Invite a client to provide a testimonial.

- ◆ Read a recent testimonial in the form of a thank-you letter.

- ◆ Show a video that highlights your most recent successes.

The most compelling story I've ever heard was told by one of my clients several years ago. The founding executive director started the organization to help find a cure for his dying wife and, in doing so, saved not just her life but the lives of many others as well. The way he told that story would bring tears to your eyes and send shivers down your spine.

What's your story? What's your motivation? Do you have a passion for your organization? Do your board members? If not, it's time to reignite the passion. Create and tell your stories!

Rate Your Organization (Do You Have a Culture of Philanthropy?)

If you can say yes to at least six of the following, you likely have a culture of philanthropy at your organization. Congratulations, you're ready to raise major gifts! If not, don't be discouraged. You'll get there, but first you've got more work to do.

Check the statements you can say "yes" to:

- ❑ Every board member makes an annual gift (100 percent board participation).

- ❑ Board member recruitment includes the expectation of both donating and helping with fundraising.

- ❑ At least half of your board members are actively engaged with fundraising (participate in two or more fundraising activities every year).

- ❑ Your senior staff donates.

- ❑ Fundraising training is a budget line item.

I'm a big fan of the Association of Fundraising Professionals (AFP), and I highly recommend that you consider joining if you're not already a member. Membership has several important benefits, but right now, I want to single out the training and continuing educational opportunities that AFP provides.

I've been a member (and an active volunteer) for over fifteen years and have attended probably an average of eight monthly meetings during each one of those years. I also attend, and frequently speak at, AFP's annual international conference. However, the main reason I'm so devoted to AFP is that it has provided me with most of my formal fundraising training.

However, as with any professional association, you need to make a commitment to attend, and even volunteer, in order to receive the most benefit. Joining a committee is the fastest way to get to know senior-level people in the field. Becoming a member of AFP will be fantastic for your current organization—and for your professional development as well!

food for thought

Do You Have a Culture of Philanthropy at Your Organization?

❑ Do you have 100 percent participation (all board members make a personal gift)?

❑ Are board members recruited with the expectation of both giving and helping with fundraising?

❑ Is your executive director an important part of your fundraising team?

❑ Is fundraising an important agenda item at your annual retreat and at every board meeting?

❑ Is there a budget line item for professional development? Is it enough to provide at least minimal board and staff member training?

If you don't yet have a culture of philanthropy at your organization, what will you do to create one?

❑ Your executive director is an integral part of the development team.

❑ The annual board retreat includes development (fundraising) as a key component of the agenda.

❑ Your development committee is active and engaged and meets at least quarterly to discuss important fundraising issues and plan various fundraising campaigns.

❑ You have a discussion about fundraising at each board meeting, not just a report of what has been raised.

Too many small and medium-sized nonprofits wait until their first capital campaign to start doing face-to-face fundraising. This approach is literally backward. At the point you're thinking about a capital campaign, it's often too late to start a solid individual giving program. The time to start face-to-face fundraising for your organization is *today*, years before you consider a capital campaign. But first, you need to create a culture of philanthropy and individual giving at your organization.

As you can see, a successful fundraising program—and particularly a successful major gifts program—can't depend on the development director alone. In order to raise the most money possible, and to be able to make the biggest possible difference to your cause, everyone at your organization needs to be involved. In the case of major gifts in particular, you absolutely must have a well-trained, cohesive team that includes the development director, executive director, and every member of your board!

To Recap

◆ A culture of philanthropy is essential to successful major gift fundraising.

◆ Board and staff involvement and continuing education are keys to having a culture of philanthropy.

◆ Being able to speak passionately about your organization and the ability to tell a compelling success story are keys both to successful major gifts fundraising and to developing a culture of philanthropy.

Chapter Two

Creating Your Strategy

IN THIS CHAPTER

···→ The difference between annual and capital campaigns

···→ How major gifts fit into your annual fund

···→ The nonprofit life cycle

···→ How to determine the amount of a major gift at your organization

···→ How to create your case for support

···→ The members of your major gifts team

···→ What you need to raise major gifts, including materials and technology

···→ Sample gift acceptance policies and why such policies are important

···→ How to create a timeline and budget for major gifts

People often associate major gifts with a capital campaign, but as I've mentioned previously, it's very important to build your major gifts program well in advance of contemplating a capital campaign. In addition, major gifts are actually the easiest and most cost-effective form of supercharging your annual fund. Why wouldn't you want to include them?

After reading this book, I hope you will consider soliciting major gifts an important component of any successful annual fund drive and will work to incorporate this strategy at your organization—this year and every year.

Annual Fund versus Capital Campaigns

An annual fund is any yearly (annual) fundraising campaign that you conduct to fund your ongoing projects and operations. It's the money you raise every year, year after year, for your programs and services. This money is raised through grant writing, fundraising events, and annual fund drives (direct mail and email). You can raise more money for your annual fund—a lot more money—by incorporating individual, face-to-face fundraising into your current annual fund campaign efforts.

And, as I mentioned in the **Introduction**, incorporating major gifts into your annual fund will prepare you for the "World Series" of fundraising—a capital campaign.

What Is a Capital Campaign?

A capital campaign is used to raise funds for long-term needs. Capital campaigns are reserved for very special circumstances, like when you need a new building. However, not all capital campaigns are for brick-and-mortar projects. You can also solicit capital campaign donations for noncapital funds like scholarships and endowments.

You should consider a capital campaign only when you need to raise significantly more than your annual campaign—and it should also work in conjunction with your annual campaign. After all, you still need to pay the light bill while you're raising money for that new scholarship!

Capital versus Annual Campaigns

The best analogy I've ever heard to describe the difference between capital and annual campaigns is the typical household budget. Think of your house: Your annual fund pays the heat, electric, and water bills (programs and services) while you use capital campaign funds to fix or replace the roof (long-term needs).

Restricted versus Unrestricted

Annual fund money can be restricted or unrestricted. In other words, funds you can use for whatever you want versus monies that are designated by the donor for a particular purpose or program. As you know, your organization needs unrestricted operating funds to pay for things like administrative costs, salaries, utility bills, and rent. At the same time, these day-to-day expenses aren't "exciting" and, therefore, aren't the kinds of expenses that most donors are eager to fund.

Many donors like to restrict their gifts for use on a particular project or program. The majority of major gifts are given as restricted funds. That's one of the reasons you still need to do broader annual appeals and events—to raise the unrestricted funds that will keep your lights on while you do the work that truly excites your donors.

That said, savvy donors increasingly understand the need for operations (unrestricted) funding. Therefore, you should broach the subject with your prospective major gifts donors, as they might be interested in helping your organization with hard-to-come-by operational funding.

If you're not sure how to ask donors for unrestricted operating funds, start with your board members. They should be willing to make unrestricted gifts with the understanding that the executive director and budgeting committee will be responsible with the funds and use them wherever the organization needs them most. Besides, if you can't convince your board members to provide unrestricted donations, how will you convince anyone else?

The Nonprofit Life Cycle

You may have heard that, like everything else, a nonprofit has a life cycle. And life-cycle age often has nothing to do with the chronological age of the organization. Organizations that have been around for many years can actually be very immature with regard to many aspects, especially fundraising. Knowing where your organization is in its developmental process is important when launching a major gifts program.

When I speak with groups about fundraising, "who does what" can vary widely depending on a variety of factors. For example, in new (young) organizations, volunteers are often responsible for more of the day-to-day activities. In more mature organizations, staff members frequently assume many, if not most, of those responsibilities.

This means that the roles and responsibilities of staff at your organization will depend, in part, on how long you have been around.

Here's a guide to the general life cycle of a nonprofit organization:

Infancy

This is the "start-up" stage, which generally lasts about five years, depending on the organization's success. In this phase, most (if not all) of the tasks involved in running (and raising money for) the nonprofit are handled by volunteers. Frequently, organizations at this stage are also running on shoestring budgets and are often run by volunteers or one full-time staff member.

Adolescence

Unlike human teenagers, nonprofits are in their adolescent phase from approximately ages five through fifteen—and sometimes much, much longer. Organizations that have lasted this long generally have some reliable funding sources and solid track records with their programming. Organizations in this stage have hired additional full-time staff to help with programs and administration.

> The age of your organization doesn't necessarily have anything to do with its level of maturity. I have seen twenty-year-old organizations that are stuck in the infancy stage.
>
> Successfully developing a major gifts program will help your organization grow and mature—because with more funding, you can hire more staff and provide more programs and services.
>
>

Maturity

Maturity overlaps with adolescence. Some organizations are fully mature at ten. Others mature much later. At this stage, an organization's programs have been running successfully for more than a decade, and it usually has several established funding streams and donors. At this point, the organization will have many (more than ten) full-time staff members.

However, don't panic if you have a mature organization but have yet to solicit major gifts. You're in good company with many other small organizations! (And, remember, size doesn't necessarily have anything to do with age.) Your goal is to make certain that your organization starts to raise major gifts now so that it can grow to the next level of maturity and security.

Now that we've covered some essential definitions, let's get into the nuts and bolts of creating your major gifts fundraising strategy.

How and Why to Define "Major Gift" for Your Organization

Before you can raise major gifts, you first need to determine what constitutes a major gift to your organization.

The term "major gift" means something different at every organization. For example, when I started my career in fundraising at a battered women's shelter, we rarely received gifts (excluding grants) of over $1,000, and we considered any gift from an individual of over $5,000 a *major gift*. Our first $10,000 donation was cause for a huge celebration around the office. That was a *very major* gift!

On the other hand, when I worked at Rutgers University many moons ago, we considered a major gift any gift over $25,000. During the same time, just down the road from Rutgers was Princeton University, where gifts didn't qualify as major until they reached $100,000 or more. (By now, I'm certain that it's $1 million or more.)

If you're at a small organization that's just getting started with individual giving and major gifts, it would be ridiculous to hold your nonprofit to the standards of Princeton University—or any other university, for that matter.

So, what do you consider a "major gift" at your organization?

Remember, major gifts don't have to be over six figures to be considered "major," and they aren't only for capital campaigns.

A major gift is a gift so large (at whatever level) that it should make the person opening the mail run to the development director's office to show off the check—and that, in turn, makes the development director jump up and run to the executive director's office. In other words, the gift should excite everyone in your organization. Once you start getting a lot of checks at that level and it becomes routine, then you can move up the amount you consider a major gift.

(The term "major gift" can also apply to the amount that particular individuals are able to give. After all, a major gift for one person might not be a major gift for someone else. For example, one donor will consider $5,000 to be a major gift, while another can give ten times that amount and think nothing of it.)

But back to determining a major gift for your organization.

Be realistic yet optimistic when picking an amount. If you've never received a gift of over $1,000, $25,000 is probably too big of a stretch. You may want to start with $5,000 or less. It also depends on your donor pool, but more on that later.

To get started, run a list from your database. Start with your top ten individual donors from the past year. Don't include corporations or foundations (unless it's a family foundation, where you have a personal connection and don't need to submit an application). Look at each of your top ten donors' cumulative giving—in other words, the total amount each gave last year, including the largest gift. For example, you may have a donor who came to your gala, bought a raffle ticket, and gave $1,000 at year-end. That donor's cumulative giving for the year would be $1,500 if the gala ticket was $300 and the raffle ticket was $200.

Are most of your top donors in the same range ($1,000 to $5,000), or are there a few outliers? One or two donors who have given gifts of $5,000 or more when your next-largest donor gave only $500? These are all factors to consider when selecting an amount for your major-gift level.

After you have identified your top level of giving, have a discussion with your executive director, development staff, and key board members to determine what your organization will designate as a major gift.

It's important to set a specific major-gift level for a few reasons:

◆ Your time is valuable. (Remember, part of the point of major gift fundraising is that it's the most time- and cost-efficient method of raising funds.) You need to be able to differentiate when it's important to spend time cultivating and soliciting someone in person versus when direct mail will suffice. Is it worth your time to meet with someone in person to ask for $1,000? If not, then that's not a major gift to your organization. On the other hand, if your organization never or rarely gets gifts of $1,000, then it *is* worth your time to work on a gift of that size.

◆ You need to know what is considered a major gift in order to recognize your donors accordingly and appropriately. Will you hang a plaque for someone who gives $1,000 or list that person on your donor wall? What about on your website? Will your executive director call to say thank you? Some of these acknowledgment methods are used for lower-level donors, but some will be reserved for major donors.

> Take some time to determine what amount your organization will consider a major gift.
>
> Do this by running a list of your top ten donors to see their giving levels. Also think about what gift level would be cause for celebration and justify the time spent on an in-person visit from you and your executive director.
>
> Discuss this strategy with your executive director and board members so that everyone is on board.
>
> 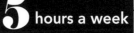 **hours a week**

Your Case for Support

Remember the storytelling I talked about in **Chapter Two** and the messaging tips I provided in **Chapter Three**? More formally, these stories are called your "case for support." Your case for support answers these questions: "Why should I give money to your organization?" and "Why should I do it now?" Your case for support revolves around those powerful personal stories about your accomplishments and is leavened with the facts and figures that prove your organization is effective. You should generally be able to state your case for support in a matter of a few pages.

Materials and Brochures

Your donor may want written materials in addition to a face-to-face meeting. If you have an annual report, written case for support, and your recent newsletter, I don't see any need for an additional "formal" brochure. In the rare instance that a donor wants more information, you can certainly provide it.

Creating Your Team

Fundraising is a team activity! It's never the sole responsibility of any one person (or at least it shouldn't be). If your boss has the attitude that you (the development director) are there to do all the fundraising, it could be time to look for another job. Your executive director and board members must be actively engaged in fundraising, especially in major gifts fundraising, alongside any development staff members.

I frequently run into development directors who say they can't raise major gifts because their executive directors aren't willing to help. If you're in that unenviable situation, try your best to work with your board members to gently remind your executive director that the success or failure of your organization (including its financial viability) ultimately rests on the executive director's shoulders. You can offer to provide training or, to make your executive director feel more comfortable, to go along on at least some ask meetings. Another good tactic is to pair your executive director with a board member you know is comfortable asking for money.

practical tip

Each person on the major gifts team has a special and distinct role. The following is best practice and theory—something to aim for. If you're not there yet—either because your organization isn't mature or experienced enough or because you have some team members who won't assume their responsibilities—you'll have to adjust.

Executive Director

The buck stops here. Ultimately, the executive director is responsible for your organization's financial success. The executive director is your organization's visionary and the person who implements the programs and services that excite donors. Therefore, your executive director needs to meet with prospective major donors on a regular basis.

Development Director

Best practice dictates that the development director is more "behind the scenes" than the executive director. The development director creates the plan, does the research, makes the appointments, and helps the executive director keep on track with major donors. Unfortunately, it doesn't always work that way, so the development director is often out meeting with donors and making asks as well.

Board Members

As we discussed in **Chapter One**, your board members are the best people to ask others for major gifts! They're volunteers, so prospects know that your board members are committed to the organization. Further, they have no financial prerogative (either real or perceived) for making the ask—unlike the executive director, whose salary comes from donations.

Gift Acceptance and Recognition Policies

Gift acceptance policies are an important part of your overall major gift strategy. These policies set ground rules for what your organization will and won't accept, and from whom. (To use an obvious example, a nonprofit dedicated to environmental protection may not want to accept a donation from an oil company!)

Not as obviously, your gift acceptance policy is there to help you avoid accepting particular gifts, even major gifts, that could end up being more trouble than they're worth in time, money, or both.

You will want to develop gift acceptance policies that work for your organization. To do so, form a committee of board members and some of your key advisors to develop a set of policies. Then have the board vote to accept them.

Here are some examples of issues that are different from organization to organization as food for thought as you move to create your own policies. For example, if you are a cancer organization, you may want to include that you won't accept gifts from tobacco companies.

You may be wondering why you wouldn't take any major gift that comes your way, but you'd be surprised at what people try to give! Here are two stories to help make my point.

When I worked at a college, one of our biggest donors wanted to give us her art collection. Unfortunately, the collection would have been more expensive for us to transport, store, and sell than we would have received for our efforts. We had to refuse her gift. She was confused and hurt, so it wasn't an easy decision, but we had our gift acceptance policies to fall back on. Fortunately, in the end, she decided to sell the art herself and donate the proceeds to the college.

Another time, a donor wanted to donate a piece of property. Unfortunately, the property was in a remote location—and actually turned out to be swampland! It would have cost the college more to accept than it was worth! We had to turn the gift down, much to the donor's disappointment.

 **stories from the real world**

Sample Gift Acceptance Policies

Here are some sample gift acceptance policies to provide your organization guidance with soliciting, receiving, and accepting major gifts. Use these as a guide as you develop your own policies.

1. Outright gifts and pledges of cash and stock will be accepted.

2. Stock will be sold within twenty-four business hours of receipt. Stock donations will be recognized at the average of the high and low value of the shares on the day of the donation.

3. Gifts of prepaid life insurance will be accepted.

4. All gifts of real estate must be approved by the executive committee before acceptance.

5. Gifts-in-kind of new technology, equipment, and furniture as requested by the organization will be accepted. No unnecessary (not needed for current programs and services as determined by the executive director) gifts-in-kind will be accepted.

6. Used gifts-in-kind will not be accepted (unless approved by the executive director on a case-by-case basis).

Or, if you're a battered women's shelter, you may not want to accept gifts from firearms companies. And, obviously, you don't want to accept any gift that will end up costing your organization money!

Timeline

You may have heard that major gifts take years to come to fruition. While that is frequently the case during capital campaigns for "megagifts" (multi-million-dollar gifts) or ultimate gifts (the biggest gift a donor makes in a lifetime) soliciting major gifts for your annual campaign should take less than a year.

As you begin your major gifts program, it's highly unlikely that you'll be soliciting mega or ultimate gifts. Remember, you're soliciting for your annual fund, so you'll be asking every year. This is important to keep in mind for a number of reasons, both to increase your annual fund revenue and to make your donors comfortable with being asked for increasingly larger amounts so that they—and you—will be ready when it's time to ask for a capital campaign-sized gift.

Regardless of the time frame, all major gifts, including mega and ultimate gifts (and all your fundraising, for that matter), should go through the same cycle:

1. Identification (who are your prospective donors?): See **Chapter Five**.

2. Cultivation (relationship building): See **Chapter Nine**.

3. Solicitation (the actual ask): See **Chapter Eleven**.

4. Stewardship (the thank-you or follow-up process): See **Chapter Twelve**.

Fundraising Cycle

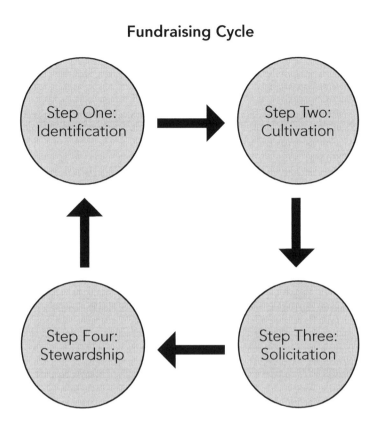

This cycle can take as little as a few weeks with someone who is very close with your organization, such as a board member. Other times, it can take much longer.

You will probably enjoy a quick cycle with your board members, who are already extremely engaged with and knowledgeable about your organization. In other words, your board members have already been identified and cultivated. You might meet with them once before asking them for a major gift and then meet again to make the ask a few weeks later.

Here's a sample timeline for a current board member or other volunteer:

◆ January—Identify the board member as a major gifts prospect; meet with the donor to cultivate and discuss the idea of a major gift.

◆ February—Sit with the prospective donor at your gala.

◆ March—Meet with the donor to ask for a major gift.

◆ April—The check arrives; "thank-you" plan is set into motion.

Total time: four months.

Donors who aren't as familiar with your organization will take longer to cultivate, but you should still ask them for a gift within one year. As I have mentioned, this is not a capital campaign and likely not a multiyear gift. If you feel you're asking too soon, ask for a slightly smaller gift and continue to cultivate so you can ask for more next year.

Depending on the maturity and development of your organization, these tasks may take a few hours, or you may need to spread them out over a few weeks. Budget them into your major gifts calendar accordingly.

◆ Create a written case for support (two to three pages). Work with board members and major donors on the final draft so you have their approval and buy-in.

◆ Develop gift acceptance policies for your organization. Recruit a subcommittee of the board to create these policies. They should be recommended by the committee and approved by the full board at your next board meeting.

◆ Create a budget for major gifts at your organization this year. You may want to wait until a little later in this book when you've created your prospect list so you can create an appropriate travel budget to reach any out-of-town prospects.

Budget

As with all development activities, it's important to have a budget for determining your planned costs associated with soliciting major gifts. It might be as small as coffee and meals with your donors, or it might even involve travel expenses if your donors aren't close geographically. Be thorough in preparing your budget so you don't experience any unpleasant surprises! And the old saying is true: It takes money to make money, so budget accordingly.

To Recap

◆ Major gifts should be part of your annual fund before your organization even considers a capital campaign.

◆ Raising major gifts requires a team effort, including the executive director, development director, and board members. Raising major gifts is not a single-person endeavor!

◆ It's important to have a formal case for support, but it's not necessary to have fancy brochures.

◆ Gift acceptance policies are an important part of your major gifts strategy.

◆ Create a timeline and budget for your major gift efforts.

Chapter Three

The Secret Weapon of Major Gifts: Engaging Your Board

IN THIS CHAPTER

···→ Why your board members are your key to success in raising major gifts

···→ How to get your board members to help with major gifts

···→ What to do when a board member just won't help

Did you know that your board of directors is the single most important factor in determining your success or failure to raise major gifts? This doesn't mean it's okay to use your board as an excuse for your own failures. What it does mean, though, is that a few "good" board members can catapult your fundraising to the next level.

The most successful campaigns that I have ever worked on have had the major support of a few key board members. That's right. A *few* key members. Not *all* of them! So don't feel disheartened if your entire board isn't made up of the most involved, effective members you can imagine (although that would be nice!) because all it really takes is a few exceptional individuals to make a significant difference.

I have never seen a campaign fail when hardworking, dedicated board members are engaged and involved.

Why Is Your Board Such an Important Factor in Major Gifts Success?

As you know, your board members play a variety of key roles for your organization. In addition, though, when it comes to fundraising, board members bring connections and credibility like few staff members can.

As we've discussed throughout this book, fundraising is about relationships. Relationships that can take months—and sometimes even years—to build. However, the members of your board already have a network of friends, family, and colleagues. These are relationships where the trust factor already exists. If your board members love your organization, it's much more likely that their friends will too. Why? Because we often share the same values as our friends—but also because friends generally trust each others' judgment.

These webs of existing relationships make your board members the best "keys" to open the doors to new potential donors. After all, if your friend asks you to meet with the executive director of an organization that she or he is excited by and committed to, it's hard to say no. If you get a call out of the blue from that same executive director without your friend's influence, though, saying no is much easier.

Board members also bring significant credibility to the table when asking for major gifts because they can genuinely say that they have put their money where their mouth is (assuming they have given first, which they should have!). There is no perception (real or otherwise) of an ulterior motive. On the other hand, when staff members (like executive directors or development directors) ask for gifts, donors might perceive that the request is for the staff member's personal benefit because the fact is that they are being paid for their work.

> I opened the paper one morning recently to find the campaign chair of one of my capital campaign clients on the front page of the business section. The story had nothing to do with my client or the campaign. But there he was, wearing his campaign pin just the same.
>
> I knew he wore the pin every day as a conversation starter (at least every time I had seen him at a campaign-related event), but there it was in black and white—proof of his dedication and commitment to this organization. It was an amazing sight! And that's not all. If this person is so dedicated to his role as campaign chair that he remembered to wear his pin for an unrelated media interview, imagine how much energy he's bringing when he's focused on the campaign!
>
> **stories from the real world**

How Can You Get Your Board to Help with Major Gifts?

There are many reasons board members give for not helping with fundraising. First and foremost (as we discussed in **Chapter One**), talking about or asking for money makes them uncomfortable. Second, they may be afraid of rejection. Third, they may have a particular discomfort with asking either friends or strangers for money. The list goes on and on, but these seem to be the big three.

What makes fundraising so uncomfortable? Sadly, many people (including board members) have an impression that raising money is about arm-twisting or—worse—begging, as I mentioned earlier. Those of us in the field, on the other hand, know that fundraising isn't about either of these things. In fact, we know that fundraising is actually about connecting people with opportunities to support causes and organizations they care about and giving them a chance to make a lasting, positive difference.

Most times (and every time when fundraising is done correctly), giving a donation makes the donor feel great. After all, how did you feel the last time you made a gift to an organization you love?

While it can be hard to change board members' false impressions about fundraising, it can and must be done. We need to change the language of raising money. Instead of thinking about just what we want the donor to do for us (or our cause), we need to talk about philanthropy as a privilege. When we ask a person to engage in philanthropy, we aren't asking for a favor. We are offering the opportunity to change (perhaps save) lives, preserve our environment, or whatever other important work your organization does on the donor's behalf.

> We need to change the language of raising money. Instead of thinking about just what we want the donor to do for us (or our cause), we need to talk about philanthropy as a privilege.
>
> When we ask a person to engage in philanthropy we aren't asking for a favor. We are offering the opportunity to change (perhaps save) lives.

important

So how do we help board members get over any fears and misperceptions they have about raising major gifts? Here are the key steps:

One Hundred Percent Participation

Your board members are the first and most important people you need to solicit for major gifts. In fact, each member should make a gift before asking anyone else for a contribution.

Remember in **Chapter One** when I talked about the importance of creating a culture of philanthropy at your organization? Encouraging, or even requiring, 100 percent participation in contributions from your board members is a key factor in the success or failure of creating such a culture.

Hopefully your board members are the closest people to your organization. They're already passionate about your mission, understand your programs and services, are familiar with your budget and needs, and are aware of any gaps in your services. If these people don't want to give to your organization, why should anyone else?

And, no, giving their time doesn't count. All too often I hear the argument, "But I give my time. Why do I have to give money too?" My answer is that your time doesn't pay the light bill or the rent. Plus, they need to lead by example.

Not only that, but your board members' willingness to give (or not) has an impact far beyond their own donations. These days, many foundations are asking about board participation. If less than 100 percent of your board members care enough to open their wallets, why should any foundations (or any other donor, for that matter) invest in your organization?

In addition, the board needs to give financially because you want and need board members to be effective advocates and fundraisers for your organization. This means that they need to be able to say "I've given my time and money, and now I'm asking for your support as well."

The old saying, "Never ask someone to do something you're not willing to do yourself," applies doubly when it comes time for board members to ask for major gifts. After all, how would you respond to someone asking you for a large sum of money when you know that person hasn't personally given a cent?

Finally, you may have noticed that I didn't discuss specific amounts for board member giving. While plenty of organizations do find success by creating a minimum gift level for board members, I feel that each member should give a gift that is significant and meaningful for that individual's own personal budget. That could be $500 for some and $10,000 (or more) for others. In order to achieve this as a goal, it will be important for each board member to be asked individually by the board chair or development committee chair—just as you would with any other donor.

> It's critical to your success with fundraising that each board member make a significant, personal contribution to your organization. Each member should be asked individually (preferably by the board chair) to give every year.
>
> **important**

What's "Give and Get?"

"Give or get" is an old fundraising term. Traditionally, it has meant that members need to either give or get money to be on the board. I (and probably many others) have changed the phrase to "Give *and* get" because I believe that board members need to help with fundraising both by giving themselves and by fundraising—or *getting*—from others. (In fundraising circles, the phrase is often expanded to "Give, get, or get off" to indicate that members who don't actively participate shouldn't be on the board at all.)

Recruit Them Right: Best Practices for Recruiting an Active, Pro-Giving, and Getting Board

One of the key ways to get board members to help with fundraising is to recruit them correctly in the first place. I cannot tell you how many organizations I've worked with that have told me they are so desperate for "bodies" on their board that they'll take anyone—and they make up-front promises that no fundraising will be involved. What!?! And then you tell me you can't get your board to raise money? Why am I not surprised?

With that in mind, here are the steps you need to take to recruit a "give and get" board:

◆ *Establish a board recruitment or nominating committee.* Every board member is responsible for identifying potential candidates, but it's this committee's job to identify places where the board needs strengthening. For example, does the board need an accountant, an attorney, someone from a corporation, or a community leader? Is the board diverse in terms of race, age, gender, geography, etc.? The committee is also responsible for vetting candidates, explaining the requirements of board service, and providing orientation to new board members.

◆ *Provide a new member orientation.* This orientation could be a two-hour session once every six months, and it might include taking the new members on a tour, introducing them to the staff, and reviewing materials like your annual report and newsletters with them. Include time to explain the various board committees, and ask them to select a committee to serve on (or let them know where they're needed most). You could also do this with each new member individually (not wait for every six months).

> Each board member should complete and sign a new expectation form each year as a way to review performance from last year and renew commitment for the coming year.
>
>
> important

◆ *Create a written job description.* Board members need job descriptions just like any other staff member does in order to fully understand what's expected of them.

◆ *Create a board member expectation form.* A board member expectation form is a simple document that outlines expectations for each board member and is signed by the member every year. It can be used in place of a written job description.

Board Retreats

Once board members are recruited and oriented properly, they should be encouraged to participate in an annual board retreat (in addition to regularly scheduled board meetings).

What's a board retreat? These occasions are full- or half-day meetings that are spent discussing and making plans for overall goals as opposed to of dealing with the normal business agenda of your board's regular meetings. The retreat is often held in a different location or setting, and it often uses an outside facilitator.

Not every organization holds board retreats, but every organization should. And many organizations that do have board retreats stay focused on strategic planning and leave fundraising off the agenda. This is a big mistake. After all, how are you going to carry out your strategic plan without money? Not only that, but your board retreats are perfect opportunities to provide fundraising training in a relaxed, no-pressure atmosphere. That's why I recommend focusing half of your retreat on strategic planning and half on raising money.

Whenever I facilitate a board retreat, I start with a call with the organization's key leaders (often the executive director, development director, and board chair) about two weeks in advance of the retreat. Because I am creating a custom agenda for them, I ask them their goals for the retreat and what they want their members to walk away from the meeting knowing and doing. Based on this conversation, I create an agenda for the day of the retreat—one that almost always includes a specific focus on fundraising.

In addition to providing training and helping set your organization's direction, these retreats are also great opportunities to reenergize your board. This is why you should include a "mission

Sample Board Member Expectation Form

Name: _____

I understand my financial commitment is necessary to ensure the success of XYZ Organization.

My company (firm) and/or I will participate in the following ways this year:

❏ Dinner gala ($100/ticket; sponsorships from $500 to $10,000) $_____

❏ Golf ($200/ticket; sponsorship opportunities from $500 to $5,000) $_____

In order to achieve 100 percent participation of the board, I personally pledge $_____

Total $_____

For my personal gift, I would prefer to make:

❏ One payment   ❏ Quarterly payments of $_____

❏ My company will match my donation. (I will submit the matching gift form with my payment(s)).

Please make gift or first pledge payment by January 31 so we can start the year with 100 percent participation.

As a board member, I agree to serve on the following committee(s) this year (check all that apply):

❏ Fundraising   ❏ Dinner gala

❏ Finance   ❏ Golf

❏ Governance   ❏ Nominating/board development

I would like to help with the following donor identification, cultivation, stewardship activities (check all that apply):

❏ Host an informational event in my home.

❏ Make thank-you calls to donors (from home or office—ten calls per year).

❏ Add personal notes to solicitations and thank-you letters (in XYZ office four times per year).

❏ Bring colleagues, friends, and family to fundraising and cultivation events.

❏ Add five or more new names to our mailing list as potential volunteers or donors.

I understand that board meeting attendance is key to the success of the board and the agency and that it is a requirement for board membership.

_____   _____

Board Member Signature   Date

moment" where you talk about a success story from the year. It's important to remind your board members why they're serving and why your organization matters. Remember, most board members aren't on the "front lines" or "in the trenches" like you are, and it's important for them to be reminded why they are there.

Once you have your board charged up and energized by your mission, talking about fundraising becomes much easier. Always include a discussion about how each member can help with fundraising in the coming year and provide fundraising training during your retreats.

Ongoing Training

As we've discussed, most people aren't natural-born fundraisers. This means that the members of your board will likely range from feeling uncomfortable with asking for money to being unwilling to do fundraising—and everything in between. Very few people are self-motivated and confident enough to go out and raise funds without some nudging, encouragement, and confidence boosting on a regular basis.

Sample Board Retreat Agenda

I recommend some version of the following agenda for your retreat:

1. Ice breaker or team-building exercise.

2. Mission moment. An activity to tug at the heartstrings of your board and remind members why they continue to serve—ideally a client discussing how his or her life has changed or a testimonial in the form of a letter, a video, etc.

3. Strategic planning (review or update strategic plan).

4. Fundraising discussion or training. (Leave ample time for this. Don't wait until end of the day!)

5. Strategic discussion about a key issue the organization is facing.

End the retreat by thanking your board members for another wonderful year of service.

Example

Therefore, it's important to have regular fundraising discussions and training sessions. I recommend that my clients include at least a fifteen-minute fundraising discussion at each board meeting. The discussion can be about prospective donors, fundraising challenges the organization or board members are facing, or planned gifts and bequests. Take time to role-play *how to ask* as well. Practice always helps!

Having regular discussions keeps raising funds a priority and is much more engaging than a boring report on your own office's fundraising activities.

Sharing Success

Another great activity for a board retreat, or even your regular meeting, is to have the members stand up and share any fundraising successes that they've had since the last

---

Plan a Board Retreat

If you don't already have an annual board retreat planned, schedule a meeting with key staff and board leaders to discuss the idea. Once you have consensus, pick a date and location. Determine whether you will use an outside facilitator. Be sure to include strategic planning and fundraising on your agenda.

to-do lists

meeting. Asking for money might not seem so intimidating if others in the room are enjoying success, and it can simulate friendly competition among board members.

The Value of Competition

There's nothing like peer pressure to get others engaged in fundraising. I've been in board rooms where the members go around the room and report what they've done since the last meeting. All action and activities are acceptable, including selling tickets to the gala, signing appeal letters, and making thank-you calls, as well as asking for major gifts. However, rounds of applause are reserved for members who report something extraordinary. This is a "soft" way to encourage them to go a bit above and beyond.

If you have a competitive board, consider giving "prizes" to members who engage in fundraising, particularly in major gifts. This could be as simple as a certificate printed in your office—or even a photo of the donor or a client with the board member. Again, the point is to change any negative perceptions about fundraising and to make asking for money something your board is willing and eager to do.

Given what you know about the people on your board, what additional creative ideas can you come up with to encourage them to raise the bar with fundraising?

Board Member Expectation Form

As I discussed in the earlier section on board recruitment, a board member expectation form is a handy way to evaluate members' performance and hold them accountable. If they haven't held up their end of the commitment by the end of the year, you can have a conversation about whether or not they wish to continue serving. If they do wish to continue, they need to consider how they'll be more involved next year.

What Do You Do When a Board Member Just Won't Help Raise Money?

Maybe you've recruited properly, provided ongoing training, held board retreats that included a focus on fundraising … and still, you have some members who just won't help raise money.

If this is still the case with your board, or if you are in the process of turning your board around as part of creating your organization's culture of philanthropy, don't be discouraged. On average, it takes three years to turn a nonfundraising board into a fundraising board—especially if members are resistant to change. To help your board get there, you need to start enforcing term limits and excusing board members from service for nonperformance. An annual review of your board member expectation form will help with that.

The Exception to the Rule: Members Who Won't Raise Money but Are Too Valuable to "Fire"

While raising money is a key board responsibility, you may have one or more members who cannot or will not fundraise but who bring significant value to your organization's mission in other ways (for example, they're experts in some aspect of your work or have significant prestige in the community). If a member fits this description and is an active and engaged volunteer in other areas, you may want to overlook the fundraising deficit. Not everyone on your board will be a superstar fundraiser, and you don't want to lose people who are actively contributing to your mission just because they are among the few who really can't raise money effectively.

How to Prevent Boring Board Meetings

If your board meetings are boring (and most I've attended are), it's no wonder you have terrible attendance and low participation. Are your meetings filled with reports—or with lively discussions?

◆ Do you provide mission moments to reconnect participants to the cause at every meeting?

◆ Do you engage your members in important policy discussions?

◆ Do you utilize their expertise?

◆ Do you provide opportunities to network with other members?

It's important to take the extra time and effort to make your board meetings worthwhile and make your members feel like they will be genuinely missed if they don't attend—and not just because you need a quorum.

To Recap

◆ Your board is the key to existing relationships—and relationships are the key to successful major gift fundraising.

◆ If you want members to raise money, you must recruit them properly, orient them well, and provide them with ongoing training.

◆ Board member expectation forms help members understand what's expected of them and help move underperforming members off the board.

◆ Board retreats should include strategic planning and fundraising training. If you have not already done so this year, plan a board retreat now.

◆ Take the time to make your regular meetings interesting and valuable to increase attendance and engagement.

Chapter Four

Building an Army of Advocates and the Role of Social Media

IN THIS CHAPTER

···→ The times are changing (constantly)—online giving's upcoming role in major gifts fundraising

···→ Social media, the ultimate peer-to-peer network

···→ Strategies for "going viral" and other tactics you can use today to increase online giving

While online giving isn't currently a reliable source of major gifts, the fact is that social media is increasingly redefining and expanding opportunities for nonprofit organizations to connect, inform, motivate, and inspire donors to give. In addition, there are increasingly frequent instances of individuals giving $10,000—or more—online.

Why is social media so important? Let's take a look at some numbers. According to an April 22, 2013, article, "12 Must-Know Stats About Social Media, Fundraising, and Cause Awareness," on nptechforgood.com, "47 percent of Americans learn about causes via social media and online channels" and "55 percent of those who engage with nonprofits via social media have been inspired to take further action."

How does this affect fundraising? Let's look at just one example—#GivingTuesday—which was first observed in 2011. #GivingTuesday is the natural outgrowth of Cyber Monday, the Monday after the start of the holiday gift-giving season when people are increasingly doing some (or even most) of their gift shopping online. During 2013's #GivingTuesday campaign, participating nonprofits raised $5 million—over four times more than was raised in 2012. In addition, the number of gifts given increased 285 percent from 2012 (and 517 percent from 2011), *and* the average gift size grew 9 percent from 2012—to $164.

Let's look at an example of what can happen when people are inspired by something they've seen or heard about online.

In June of 2012, an elderly school bus monitor in northern New York was bullied to tears by a bunch of seventh-grade students on her route. One of the bullies taped the incident and put it on YouTube.

The video went viral. Within days, literally millions of people had seen it (in fact, as I write this book, nearly nine million people have watched the video on YouTube). However, people didn't just watch and walk away. Instead, a man in Canada was moved to start a campaign on the site indiegogo.com with the goal of raising $5,000 to give the bus monitor, Karen Klein, a vacation.

You can probably guess what happened, or perhaps you saw it on the news. Ultimately, the Karen Klein fund raised more than $700,000—$100,000 of which Ms. Klein has used as seed money to start an antibullying foundation.

This story illustrates the power that can be harnessed when hundreds, thousands, or millions of people are strongly influenced to take action because of something they have seen or heard online.

stories from the real world

Of course, online giving isn't limited to events like #GivingTuesday. It happens year-round, often in unique and startling ways.

The Klein story is a great example of the fact that the Internet eliminates the geographic boundaries that have traditionally limited the reach of nonprofits, particularly small shops. Thanks to the Internet, after all, a Canadian citizen was moved by the plight of an elderly woman in the United States! Similarly, it is now possible for your nonprofit shelter for abused and abandoned horses (for example) to receive gifts from horse lovers who live across the continent (or even across the ocean) from your location.

It sounds wonderful, doesn't it? Just tell a compelling story, put that story online, and wait for the money to pour in. Sadly, it's not that simple. For every Karen Klein, there are thousands, if not tens of thousands, of equally important stories that have not reached anywhere near a critical mass of reaction. Why? *Because there are tens of thousands of them,* plus all the other messages in all the other media that are competing for our attention.

In other words, putting all your efforts into online fundraising and expecting a $500,000 or more payout isn't much more reliable than spending a large chunk of your household budget on lottery tickets.

There is also an uglier side to the Karen Klein story. While thousands of people were moved to do a kind thing for an elderly woman who was unjustly bullied, others chose instead to harass her bullies, including publishing their names online and sending death threats. While your nonprofit organization will almost certainly never need to worry about encountering such a violently negative reaction to your online efforts, this side of the Klein story is a strong reminder of one of the most important concepts of online communication: When you choose to communicate or fundraise online, your story quickly becomes the "property" of your audience. You can shape the conversations that result, but you can't control them.

Given the relative unreliability and unpredictability of online communications and fundraising, why should your small nonprofit implement an online (including social media) strategy? Because even with the drawbacks I've outlined above, online fundraising does work, including when it comes to raising major gifts.

Of course, generally you need to do more than communicate with people online before they'll give a major gift, but it's certainly one of the tools in your fundraising toolbox.

Not only that, but today's young people—who will eventually become tomorrow's major donors—are increasingly learning about and engaging with nonprofit organizations online.

Let's take a look at some facts about online fundraising today.

According to Blackbaud's 2011 Online Giving Report, 87 percent of the 1,874 surveyed organizations had received at least one gift of $1,000 or more online. The largest online gift was (I hope you're sitting down while you're reading this) $260,000!

When you think about it, the trend of giving larger amounts online makes sense. Amazon has been with us since 1994, and eBay was born just a year later. Today you can buy virtually anything online, including big-ticket items like cars, vacations, and expensive jewelry. Given that people are becoming accustomed to spending higher amounts of money online as consumers, it makes sense that they're also becoming more comfortable doing the same thing in their role as donors.

Another fantastic thing about online fundraising is that it can help level the playing field. Again according to Blackbaud, small nonprofits (with annual budgets of less than $1 million) saw an increase in online giving of 12.8 percent in 2011. Medium-sized nonprofits ($1 million to $10 million) experienced a 13.1 percent increase, and large organizations (more than $10 million) realized only 8.6 percent growth. Granted, your organization needs to dedicate time and effort to online fundraising to make it work. You can't just stick a "donate" button on your website and expect to get results. But at least so far, it looks like small nonprofits have a solid opportunity when it comes to succeeding with online giving.

Remember earlier in the book when I outlined the role of direct mail? The fact is, within the next ten to twenty years, direct mail will be out—and nonprofits will need to make up that revenue somewhere. More often than not, those revenues (and the other benefits of direct mail, like identifying potential major donors) will come from online sources.

Social Media, the Ultimate Peer-to-Peer Network

We've already discussed the importance of peer-to-peer fundraising in terms of major gifts. Every part of the major gift asking process, in fact, is designed to create the relationships that make people feel good about getting out their checkbooks and making gifts to your organization.

The main reason you need to start thinking about and implementing effective online giving programs and integrating social media into your overall fundraising strategy now is to make sure you're ready for the future of giving. If you need convincing, here is some data from "The Next Generation of Online Giving," a survey by Pam Loeb, Gayle Vogel, and Emily Hahn of Edge Research:

◆ While the cohorts that the study's authors call "Matures" (born in 1945 or before) and (of course) the baby boomers (born from 1946 through 1964) report giving the most to charities of any of the populations surveyed, they also report having first learned about the top charities that they support today while in their thirties. Guess which generation is in or entering its thirties now? Generation Y (born from 1981 through 1995), a generation that is coming of age in an online world.

◆ Meanwhile, generation X (born 1965 through 1980) is still figuring out which causes and organizations it cares about. But, like generation Y, this generation uses social media for news and to show support for—and donate to—nonprofit organizations.

◆ Finally, while you may think of baby boomers as being more traditional givers, the survey's authors say, "Boomers' online giving and social media usage shot up since we last checked in with them in 2010. In fact, Boomers seem to be the transitional generation—the last one where direct mail will do the heavy lifting."

As you're probably aware, online giving is no different. Donors are much more likely to make gifts because friends have asked them to give. And this is exactly where social media sites like Facebook, LinkedIn, Pinterest, and others come into the picture.

Just how influential can social media be? Let's go back to the story about Karen Klein. According to the September 28, 2012, article in the *Stanford Social Innovation Review* about her story, "During the first nine days [after the video was posted], her story lit-up Twitter with over 21,000 mentions. The 'tweets' peaked during the first two days, then blogs, forums, and traditional media picked up the story, and shared it some 8,400 more times." Thanks to all that attention, it took only seven days to raise the more than $700,000 Ms. Klein ultimately received.

It isn't the place of this book to give you any kind of complete overview of the role of social media in online giving. For one thing, there are already literally hundreds of books, blog posts, and online articles by people in both the nonprofit and for-profit worlds who are studying the ins and outs of making social media work as a marketing, communications, and fundraising tool. In the next section of this chapter, I'll give you a few quick tips about things you can start doing today to increase your online giving. In the meantime, after you have gotten your major gifts program up and running, I strongly suggest that you turn part of your attention to social media tools.

Before we move on, however, I'd like to elaborate just a bit about a point I made above: When you use traditional messaging channels, like print, television, or radio, you control the message. On social media, though, the audience does. To give you just one example, in November 2013, JP Morgan

Chase, an investment bank that has been targeted for its role in the 2008 recession, decided to launch #AskJPM on Twitter. The idea was to encourage users to Tweet financial career-related questions to the bank's Vice Chairman, James Lee.

Less than six hours later, the bank literally retreated in the face of more than six thousand responses, most of which were overwhelmingly negative. One example, sent by someone with the user name @moneymcbags, said: "How many $jpm bankers does it take to screw in a light bulb? None, they just foreclose on the house."

While you may not have heard about the JP Morgan online tsunami, let's look at a case that's closer to home: the massive public outcry, including literally thousands of negative posts on its Facebook page alone, when the Susan G. Komen Foundation announced that it was cutting out a grant to Planned Parenthood for breast cancer screenings. While the news was originally announced through traditional media—in this case, the Associated Press—largely as a result of the social media outcry (and Planned Parenthood's wise use of social media forums), Planned Parenthood received "hundreds of thousands" of donations in the span of just twenty-four hours after the Komen announcement, according to a February 1, 2012, report on *The Huffington Post*. This was in addition to a gift of $250,000 from a well-off Texas couple. (A May 27, 2012, report in *The Chronicle of Philanthropy* stated that Planned Parenthood's Breast Health Emergency Fund eventually raised more than $3 million!) As you may know, Komen for the Cure also reversed its decision and reinstated the grant.

Given the common idea that the Internet has a short attention span, you may think that Komen has recovered from the Planned Parenthood controversy. In fact, the reverse is true. A July 5, 2013, report in *The National Catholic Register* said that the Komen foundation canceled its famous three-day fundraising walks in seven cities due to declining participation.

Regardless of how you may feel about the their organizations and missions, the Komen for the Cure/Planned Parenthood controversy is an excellent example of the power and influence that social media can have on nonprofit organizations.

There are a few important points for nonprofits to take away from the Karen Klein, JP Morgan, Komen/Planned Parenthood, and hundreds of other accounts of the wonderful and sometimes very scary turn that messages can take once they've been turned loose on the Internet:

◆ Roll with it! Encourage your online supporters to make your story theirs as they share it with their friends. Don't hesitate to chime in on the discussion with polite corrections if someone gets a fact about your organization wrong, but otherwise do everything you can to be a cheerleader for those who feel inspired to share your nonprofit with their friends.

◆ If you make a mistake (online or off line), issue a sincere apology. Whatever you do, don't become defensive. That's the quickest and easiest way to attract exactly the kind of attention you don't want!

◆ "Listen." Donors and supporters won't just share news about you and give money to you. They'll also share ideas with you about the things they'd like to see your organization do. You certainly don't have to implement every suggestion you receive online. In fact, many if not most of them will probably be things your organization can't or doesn't want to do. However, you do need to acknowledge and thank everyone who cares enough to write in with an idea.

◆ "Likes" do matter. On one hand, a "Like" on Facebook doesn't put money into your bank account. It isn't a signature on a petition, a blanket you can give to a homeless person, or a can of food for a puppy. On the other, you have no idea how many people will see someone's "Like" and decide to check out (and potentially give to) your organization.

Those who care enough to engage with your organization online should be treated like the VIPs that they are. Try to bring the engagement off line and in person. They could be major gift prospects.

Strategies for "Going Viral" and Other Tactics You Can Use Today to Increase Online Giving

In addition to thinking of your social media messaging as a wave you're riding rather than a show you're directing, there are several other things you can do to successfully encourage people to engage with and give to your nonprofit via online channels.

Again, this is a topic that could take up an entire book by itself. And, again, I strongly recommend that you make sure your major gifts program is well established before spending a lot of time with online giving. That said, here are a few things you can do to increase the amount of money you raise online:

◆ Make it easy. This seems obvious, but you'd be surprised how many nonprofit organizations make it difficult to either give online or figure out how to make an off-line gift. What do I mean by "make it easy"? For one thing, your mailing address should appear not just on your "contact" page but also at the bottom of the main page of your website so those who want to write and send checks don't have to search for that information. In addition, make sure your "donate online" button is obvious and leads to a donation form that is easy to fill out—and doesn't ask for any personal information other than what's needed to process the donation.

◆ Donors give with their hearts, not their heads, and this is particularly true online. Yes, you need to make sure that potential supporters can learn the facts about your organization on your website, but you also need to put your emotional appeal front and center, right there on your home page. If possible, include video testimonials and stories.

◆ How can you make one of your blog posts or videos go viral? You can't. What you *can* do is create content that is more likely to go viral because it stirs strong emotions. If you can make people laugh out loud, cry, feel outraged, or feel the urgency of your cause, they are much more likely to not only share your content but also recommend it to their friends. The key here is strong emotions. People don't share content that makes them chuckle or feel slightly sad.

◆ Thank your supporters, and thank them far and wide. Just as you always send thank-you letters and other recognition to your traditional donors and supporters, it's vitally important to recognize your online donors and supporters. Did Joe Smith share your petition with five hundred friends? A quick Tweet or pat on the back on Facebook won't take much time, but it will encourage Joe Smith (and his friends) to do even more. However, always check with donors first to find out if they are willing to be thanked publicly.

◆ As soon as you have the funds available to do so, make sure that your website and blog are designed to look good on tablets and mobile phones as well as on laptop and desktop computers. If you have a smartphone, think about it – how often do you give up (quickly) on a website that's difficult to navigate on your phone? Well, so does everyone else. And, as we all know, smartphones and tablets are becoming increasingly popular, particularly with the younger donors who are your future major gift patrons.

Engage Donors and Followers through Social Media

◆ Update your website so that your "donate now" button is clearly visible and accessible from all pages. Your donation page should be simple and clear and should collect only the information that's necessary for the donation.

◆ Create compelling content that people will want to share—stories that move them to laughter or tears.

◆ Upgrade your website to make sure it is easy to read on mobile devices.

 to-do lists

---

As much as you may feel the Internet is "impersonal" and does not have a place in major gifts, that simply isn't true. People in every generation are turning to the Internet to maintain and strengthen relationships with family and friends because social media makes it easy to keep in touch on a regular and ongoing basis.

Social media and online giving are playing an increasingly important role in the way we communicate with one another and, therefore, for fundraising and major gifts. Although online giving should not be your number-one priority in terms of raising major gifts, it is important to ensure that your website and social media channels are up to date and easy to use.

To Recap

◆ Social media and the Internet have a role to play in major gifts in terms of keeping donors connected and engaged.

◆ Donors are becoming increasingly likely to make major gifts online.

◆ Social media is the ultimate peer-to-peer network, and it will be increasingly more important to connect with younger donors and future major gifts prospects through this medium.

Chapter Five

What Does Bulk Mail Have to Do with Major Gifts?

IN THIS CHAPTER

- ···➔ How direct mail helps identify major gift donors

- ···➔ Snail mail—why it's still relevant

- ···➔ Tell a great story!

- ···➔ Why it's important to create personalized, donor-focused bulk mail

- ···➔ Online giving and email solicitation

- ···➔ Your database—a key to successful major gift fundraising

- ···➔ When you should, and should not, send mail to your major gifts donors

While I didn't intend to write a chapter on direct mail, this strategy is too critical to your major gifts efforts to be left out.

Why? Because bulk mail, whether traditional postal ("snail") mail or email, is an opportunity for individuals to self-identify as being interested in your cause. When individuals reply to your mailing with a donation, it's like they're raising their hands to let you know you're important to them. If they do it again or repeatedly, you know they are *very* interested in your cause.

This process of self-identification helps you easily find people who are already impressed enough by your organization to open their checkbooks—and, therefore, helps you identify some of your best prospects for major gifts.

Bulk mail is any formal solicitation (or request for donations) that is sent by mail—whether snail mail or email—and has a built-in reply mechanism for the donor, such as a reply envelope or "donate now" button.

Snail Mail—Why It's Still Relevant

Think snail mail is too expensive and not worth doing? Are you considering abandoning the post office altogether? If so, think again: Snail mail serves a variety of purposes and is far from extinct.

Although it's an expensive form of fundraising (and if not done properly can have a negative net), bulk postal mail is still an important component of your overall fundraising program and should be paid the attention it deserves. (Admittedly, I may change my mind in the next five or ten years, but for now, direct mail still has an important role to play in the fundraising world.) When done well, direct mail is a great source of unrestricted operating revenue in addition to its role of identifying prospective major gift donors!

Online contributions work the same way as bulk mail—they generate operating revenue, *and* they're a fantastic way to identify major gift prospects. When people care enough to click and give, with time and proper stewardship, they are more likely to want to meet in person—and give much more.

It's also important to note that bulk mail and the Internet are not an either/or proposition: You can and should make the two work together. Assuming you're able to accept donations online, use the "PS" at the end of your bulk mail solicitation letter to encourage people to donate via your website. Here's an example:

PS: We hope you will consider joining our Givers Club for as little as ten dollars per month. Check out the video on our website at abcorganization.org for more important details about how we help save whales, and please consider making your donation online.

Tell a Great Story

Impactful, moving stories aren't just a way to inspire passion in your board. They also belong in your appeal letters. For example, think about *The Diary of Anne Frank,* which is a fantastic example of the kind of story I'm talking about. Why? Because it's hard for most people to take in the fact that six million people died in the Holocaust. Six million is an unimaginably large number! But the story of a child suffering through the Holocaust, told in her own words? Suddenly, the situation becomes brutally real.

PS: Your "PS" Matters

If you're not ending your donation letters with a "PS," you need to start. Believe it or not, many people will skip your entire letter (no matter how well written) and go directly to the PS because it stands out.

Don't miss this important opportunity. Make your PS an effective call to action!

Anne Frank's story is related to your fundraising appeal because in order to inspire donors to give, you need to share a personal story your potential donors can relate to—a story that will capture their attention and touch their hearts.

Your story isn't about the facts and figures of your accomplishments, although you can and should include a few facts and figures in your letter. Instead, focus on the story of one person you've helped this year, or one of the tracts of wetlands you've saved this year, or...

In other words, make your solicitation letter personal, because giving is one of the most personal of decisions.

You can use quotes and testimonials too. Nothing "sells" an organization like the personal testimonies of others!

Why It's Important to Create Personalized, Donor-Focused Bulk Mail

Do you think the envelope of your bulk mail piece is irrelevant? If so, you're sadly mistaken. Think about it this way: If the envelope doesn't get opened, it doesn't matter how good your letter is. The goal of bulk mail today is to be as unlike old-style bulk mail as possible. How do you achieve this? By making your bulk mail look like what it is: a personalized message to each individual who receives it. Here are some ways to personalize your bulk mail envelopes:

◆ Use a "live" stamp. Nothing says "bulk mail" like a postage metered letter.

◆ Hand address the envelope. This takes extra time, but it can be done for your top donors.

◆ Add the name of a board member above the return address.

Once a potential reader has opened the envelope, it's certainly not time to go all bulk mail on them. Does your letter say "Dear Friend" or "Dear Sally?" (If your donors or organization are more formal in nature, then "Mrs. Smith" is also appropriate, but *never* "Dear Friend!" Today's technology makes it so easy to personalize letters that there is no excuse not to do so with your all-important appeal letter!

It's the same with email. The subject line and the sender's address matter! Think about it. Are you more likely to open email from a friend or from an organization? Can your online appeals come from board members to their contact lists to improve your open rates?

How can you make your snail mail and email appeals as personal as possible so that your recipients open and read them?

The Letter Isn't About You (or Your Organization)!

This may seem counterintuitive, but this is the century of donor-focused fundraising. This means that the letter should be about the donor, not about your organization.

> ### Focus on the Donor, Not the Organization, in Your Appeal Letter
>
> Instead of: "This year, we helped 150 children succeed in school through our after-school programs."
>
> Write this: "This year, you helped 150 children succeed in school, thanks to your generous support of our after-school program."
>
>

No one explains this better than my colleague and mentor Tom Ahern, who recommends comparing the number of times you use "I" (and "we") with the number of times you use "you" in your letter. If you cut down on the excessive use of "I" and "we"—and use "you" more often—you will have a letter that's focused on the donor, not on the organization.

Do You Accept Credit Cards Online?

If you're not using email to solicit your donors, you haven't joined the twenty-first century. It's time to get with the times! Donors, including major donors, are increasingly turning to the web to make their gifts. In a few short years, I'd guess that a majority of giving is going to be done online.

Make giving to your organization as simple as clicking a link on every email, and you've increased the likelihood of a response severalfold.

Another reason to make certain your donors can give online is that even donors who are getting your snail-mail letters may be more and more likely to go to their computers, not to their checkbooks, to make their gifts!

At a minimum, you should be able to accept credit card gifts using a low-cost service like PayPal. Ideally, though, you'd be able to accept credit cards through a service that is integrated with your website so that donors feel like they are on your site while making their donations. I'm not suggesting that you spend a lot of money on a credit card donation system, but ideally you'll invest in making it possible for donors to give via a page on your website. If you use an outside service, you should have your own customized page on that service that has the same "look and feel" as your site.

Email

Once you have your credit card donation system set up, it's time to start soliciting donors online via email. But these aren't the same letters you send by postal mail. Can you

> ### Work on Your Appeal Letters
>
> Take five hours to work on your appeal letters—both email and snail mail—for this year. Don't believe you can develop a theme, identify a testimonial, dig up great statistics, and write a letter in just five hours? Well, it took me less than five hours to write this chapter, so I know you can write your appeal letter (or at least a solid first draft) in that amount of time if you sit down and put your mind to it!
>
> Depending on what time of year you start this book, it might feel odd to be writing your appeal letters now, but you'll be glad you did when the time comes to send them.
>
> **5 hours a week**

imagine receiving a four-page letter via email? Donors never scroll down that far. That's just too long!

In contrast with your snail-mail letters, your email solicitation should be short and to the point—only one screen shot long (or about five hundred words) if possible. (You can still use the same theme or story as your snail-mail appeal. Just use a condensed version.) Your email can contain links to additional information, but the one and only link that you want people to follow is the "donate now" button. Make sure you highlight that button and place it at both the top and bottom of your email solicitation right next to a strong "call to action" to donate.

Your Database—A Key to Successful Major Gift Fundraising

Let's say you have a great direct mail program or great events but you haven't developed a great system for capturing donor histories. As a result, you don't have an adequate database. Or perhaps you don't have any database yet. If that's the case, it's time to get serious about keeping those records! You need a database—a computerized method of keeping donor records—and you need it right away if you're serious about fundraising and soliciting major gifts.

There are many great fundraising programs on the market to choose from, including databases designed specifically for fundraising and larger programs that include databases. The available software ranges in price from affordable to expensive. At this point, while you're growing your list, I don't recommend the most expensive products on the market. In fact, if you're well versed in Microsoft Access or another database product, you can use that until you decide it's necessary to invest in specialized fundraising software. (By the way, for those of you who don't know the difference, Microsoft Excel is *not* a database! Please don't pretend it *is* one.)

Not only do you need a database, but it's also vital that you keep it up to date and capturing the information you need, including:

◆ Name (first and last of each spouse or partner).

◆ Address (home and office, if appropriate).

◆ Email address. (If you haven't already started collecting email addresses, this is critical for email solicitations.)

◆ Phone number(s) (home office, cell).

◆ Giving history (responses to each appeal, ticket purchases, etc.).

◆ Relationships. (Who do they know at your organizations? This is important if they have existing relationships with your board members.)

◆ Notes (great place to put things you've learned after a meeting with your donor).

Why is this so important? Remember all those donors who are signaling their interest in your organization by responding to your appeals? Capturing their data and giving history is essential

While it's important to keep notes on your major and other donors, don't put anything in your donor database that you wouldn't want your donor to see. Donors have the right to request their donor files at any time. A good rule of thumb is to stick to the facts. And don't include anything that would be embarrassing to your donor.

for figuring out which ones among them are good major gift prospects. I'll get into more specifics about how to use your data to sift for major donor prospects in **Chapter Five**, but this needs to be said here as well.

In addition to identifying information and giving histories, you will also want to capture information about your donors after you meet with them, including a summary of your conversations. Make note of useful pieces of information, such as what program(s) they are especially interested in, why they started giving to your organization in the first place, what keeps them giving, and what they like and dislike about your organization. It's also critical to note what the next steps are with each particular donor. After all, this is (hopefully) leading to a major gift. You can also make note of facts—like a recent divorce or a job loss—but keep all judgment out of your notes. Remember, donors can request to see their own files, so be aware of that as you make notes about them. Don't write anything you wouldn't want them to see!

One further note about your database: Have you heard the expression "garbage in, garbage out"? If you're not maintaining "clean" (correct) data, then your database won't do you any good. Assign someone other than the person doing data entry to spot check for errors on a regular basis. Are gifts being entered and coded correctly? If someone moves, who is responsible for updating the database?

Your donor database is so important because it captures the results of your direct mail efforts, events, and interactions with your donors. This will be an invaluable tool for you as you move forward with major gifts.

Should You Send Bulk Mail to Your Major Gifts Donors?

I'm frequently asked whether or not to pull major gifts prospects out of the annual appeal pool. In most cases, my answer is no. Here's why: Imagine you pull your top ten donors

Evaluate and spot-check your database on a regular basis. Are you collecting all the information you need, including contact information (address, email address, phone numbers) and donor history (how much each contact has given historically for each event or appeal)?

Also, spot-check gifts to make sure they are entered correctly on a regular, ongoing basis. (I recommend monthly, unless you are getting an extraordinarily high number of gifts, like at year-end, when you can check more often.) Someone other than the person doing the data entry should be the one spot-checking. Avoid "garbage in" now, and you won't have "garbage out" later.

If your database is inadequate for capturing and filtering information about your best and biggest donors, it's time to research new options.

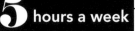

from receiving the annual appeal letter because you want to ask them for a major gift in person. However, one thing after another gets in your way of having those meetings. Now, the end of the year is here, and you haven't asked for gifts in person. *And* they haven't received your annual letter! Now, your top ten donors haven't been asked for gifts and, therefore, don't make gifts this year.

The only time I would pull a major donor from a mail (or email) appeal list is if I have an appointment to meet that individual in the same month that the mailing is going out. I also make a note on my calendar to add the major donor back to the mailing list in the event our meeting is canceled or postponed.

To Recap

◆ Bulk mail plays an important role in helping identify major gifts prospects.

◆ It's still important to use traditional mail as well as email to solicit your donors.

◆ Be donor focused and personalize all solicitation letters for the best response.

◆ Your donor database is vital for identifying major gifts prospects.

◆ Spot-check your database for accuracy.

◆ Pull major donors out of bulk mail appeals only if your meeting with them is imminent.

Part Two

Are You Ready to Ask for Major Gifts? Preparing to Ask

Part Two covers everything from identifying your prospective major donors to building relationships with them—everything that needs to happen prior to asking. The first step in the fundraising cycle is identifying who you will try to raise major gifts from, and it takes you through the process of making a list of twenty individuals. You will also learn why it is important to understand as much as you can about those individuals while also being ethical. And, once you have your researched list, it's time to get to know those individuals and meet with them. The second stage of the fundraising cycle is building relationships with your prospective donors. And, since fundraising is about relationships, you will learn exactly how to build those relationships prior to asking for major gifts.

Chapter Six

Who Will You Ask for Major Gifts?

IN THIS CHAPTER

- ---→ Why your database is key to raising major gifts

- ---→ How to identify prospective donors for major gifts

- ---→ How to search your database for major gift donors

- ---→ Why low-level, loyal donors are important to your major gifts program

- ---→ What to do if you don't have a donor history or database

Obviously, you need to identify who you're going to ask before you can raise money from them. So where will you find your prospective major gift donors? As we talked about in **Chapter Three**, the first place you'll find them is in your current pool of donors—people who have already demonstrated that they're interested enough in your cause to open their checkbooks for you.

I see too many people at nonprofit organizations waste their time looking for new donors when they have a great pool of people to pull from who are already committed to their organization and cause!

I'm not suggesting that you stop cultivating new donors. There's certainly a need for new names and faces, but in order to start your major gift program, we're going to start with tried and true.

Fundraising Cycle—Step One: Identification

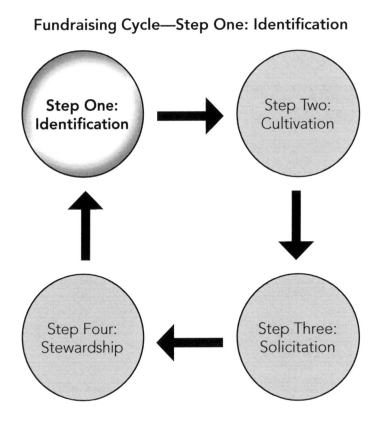

Why Your Database Is Key to Raising Major Gifts

As I discussed earlier, a donor database is where you keep contact information and a history of donation records for all your supporters and prospects. A well-kept, up-to-date donor database is one of the most important tools you need to help organize your fundraising efforts, including major gift donors.

We've already touched on the importance of databases. In **Chapter Two**, you used your database to determine the amount that counts as a major gift for your organization. And in **Chapter Three**, we talked about your database in conjunction with direct mail.

The information you keep in your database is critical to your success, because you use it for everything from sending out accurately addressed and personalized bulk mail to identifying prospective donors for major gift fundraising based on their giving history and relationship with your organization.

Your database isn't just for storage—you must also be able to query it and run reports to accurately sort information, particularly when you're looking for prospective major gift donors.

Remember the phrase "garbage in, garbage out"? That means that your data is only as good as it is accurate. How do you feel when you receive solicitations or other mail with your name misspelled? Your donors feel the same way. And the more they have received, the more likely they are to be offended. This is why it's vitally important to have your information audited for accuracy on a fairly regular basis, as we already covered earlier.

You May Already Have Major Donors in Your Database!

Remember in **Chapter Two** when you determined the amount that constitutes a major gift for your organization? While you were doing so, you may have identified a few donors who have already given major gifts—or amounts close to major gifts. But whether or not you've already identified major contributors in your database, it's now time to run reports to find the two most important types of donors—the ones who have given the largest amounts, and the ones who have given repeatedly over time. If you're really lucky, these two groups will overlap and many of your largest donors will also be your most loyal.

Large Donors

Run a report of your biggest donors from last year. Use cumulative giving so that you're certain to capture any donors who make regular, small donations throughout the year that add up to major amounts. Include every donation, including ticket purchases (event and raffle), responses to appeals, online gifts, etc., in your report.

You can also run a report for "lifetime giving," meaning the total that individual donors have given during their entire relationship with your organization. The lifetime giving report will ensure you won't miss anyone who didn't give, or gave a smaller amount for any reason, last year but should still be on your biggest donor list.

Loyal Donors

Loyal donors are those individuals who give year after year, regardless of the amount. They're the people who have given seven or more times over the last ten years. (Don't exclude donors simply because they have skipped a year or two. A lapse may be an accident or the result of a major life event, not because a donor is inconsistent or uncaring.)

It's important to have a list of loyal donors, regardless of the amount of their individual gifts, even donors who give only ten dollars per year. These loyal donors are important because they already believe in your cause and love your organization. With a little attention and VIP treatment, they could become some of your largest donors. And even if they can't make major gifts right away, they are fantastic planned giving prospects.

Whittling Your List

After you've run a list of your largest donors and your most loyal donors, go through the lists and remove corporations and foundations. The only foundations you should leave are the foundations of individuals or families that don't require you to submit an application or other formal paperwork.

After you remove the corporations and foundations, the list could be very small. If that's the case, you may need to go back and rerun the largest donors list to include lower-level donors.

One of the biggest mistakes that development staff members make when trying to fundraise from individuals is not keeping a list of specific prospects. Instead, they try to cultivate

Focus your efforts where they will do your organization the most good. Use the 90/10 rule—90 percent of your fundraising income will come from the top 10 percent of your donors. Way too often, I see development officers spending 90 percent of their time on the bottom 10 percent of their donors—and that leads to bad results.

everyone—every single person they come in contact with! If you've ever felt like your work has you on a "hamster wheel," it could be that you're one of those fundraisers who falls into the "cultivate everyone" camp.

But if you're going to truly get in the major gift game, you will need to learn how to focus on a small handful of highly rated, highly committed prospective donors. After all, you have only a small amount of time to commit to this (five hours per week), assuming you're doing everything else in the development office as well.

At any given moment, you should be able to name your top prospects and some key facts about them. Start considering them as part of your list of personal business contacts, if not your friends. Once you start cultivating them (we'll get to that in a later chapter), you should get to know them—and they should get to know you—well enough that they answer your calls and return your emails no matter how high up they are in their companies.

When you run your reports on your largest and most loyal donors, your ultimate goal is to come up with a list of your twenty best major gift prospects. Pin this list up over your desk and review it every day.

How will you come up with these first twenty prospects? Follow these steps:

1. Start with the two lists you ran earlier from your database—your largest and most loyal donors lists. Hopefully, there are a lot of names on these lists (at least more than twenty). Start with the highest donors on your list, even if they have only given one hundred dollars per year. You need to start somewhere.

2. Delete the corporations and foundations from your list. I realize that this will potentially eliminate most of the large donors from your list. If so, run more lists.

3. Merge the lists. Take anyone who appears on both lists (your largest and most loyal), and move them to the top of your list. This is the beginning of your "A" list of prospects.

Identify people who have both *capacity* and *inclination* as your top-level prospects.

Capacity refers to one's ability to give financial resources.

Inclination refers to one's interest in the organization, mission, or cause.

4.   Take your lists to a meeting with your top staff, key board and development committee members. Discuss each name on your list with the end goal in mind of developing a tight list of twenty of your best prospective major gift donors.

In the meeting with staff and board members, rate each person on the list based on what you and others in the room know about the individual. Consider individual capacity and inclination. In addition to their donations, do these people show an interest in your organization by attending events or volunteering? Do you know what they do for a living and how they live? Do they take lavish vacations, live in fancy houses, etc.?

Here's a basic rating system to use during this meeting. Feel free to create your own, but don't make it overly complicated. Rate each person on your lists:

Inclination (in Your Organization)

1 = extremely interested

2 = interested

3 = unsure

Capacity

A = wealthy (could donate $100,000 or more)

B = upper middle class (could donate $5,000 or more)

C = working class (could donate $1,000 or more)

D = poor (could not donate $1,000)

These may seem like high numbers, but we're not talking about bulk mail here. We're talking about major gifts!

Move your A-1s to the top of your list.

> ## Identify Your Major Gifts Prospects: Create a "Top-Twenty" List
>
> Run two lists from your database. The first list is of your largest donors, and the second of your most loyal donors. Eliminate corporations and foundations from your lists. After all, we're looking to grow major gifts from individual donors. Then compare lists and make a note of those who appear on both lists. Those individuals are your *best* donors—large and loyal! Form a committee to rate the remaining individuals so you can whittle your list to your top twenty prospective major gifts donors.
>
> Or…
>
> If you don't have a donor database, meet with your top staff and board members to develop your top twenty "friendraising" list.
>
>

The Importance of the B List

Unfortunately, not everyone on your top-twenty list (A-1 list) will meet with you or donate because some may move away, pass away, or experience significant major life events (death in the family, loss of a job) that will impact their ability to make major gifts or any further major gifts if they have already done so.

During your prospect rating meeting, therefore, you'll want to develop a "B" list as well. When people drop off the A list, move someone from the B list up. The goal is to have twenty people on your prospect list at all times.

Loyal Donors Are Important Too

Remember that not all of your most loyal donors will necessarily end up on your A-1 list. At first, in fact, very few may do so. These people are obviously interested in your cause and philanthropic, but the reason they're giving only regular small amounts is that may be all they can do. That's fine too.

Keep them on your annual fund list, and keep sending them mailings and inviting them to events. They are not your best individual major gift prospects. At least not right now. But, as your most loyal donors, they are VIPs to your organization and your number-one prospects for planned gifts. More on that in the chapter about planned gifts.

No Database? No Problem (Friendraising)

If you don't have any donor data or history, you still need to make a list before you can get started raising major gifts.

How do you create this list? Start by asking board and staff members to identify people they know. Emphasize the fact that at this stage you are friendraising, not fundraising, for the organization and that you want to grow your list of supporters at all levels. In other words, the people they suggest need not be "rich." If you ask for a list of only wealthy people, you will be where you started—nowhere!

Are you more likely to make a donation if a friend asks or if you get a call or letter from an organization directly?

I assume you said you're much more likely to give if a friend asks, because it's true. You are more likely to give when a friend asks because you trust your friend, and that trust is carried forward to the organization that your friend is recommending.

Remember, fundraising is all about relationships—and trust—which is why we always want to start with people we know.

I do the following exercise whenever I facilitate a board retreat where one of the objectives is to help board members identify prospective donors for the organization: First, I draw a circle with spokes of a wheel, and in the center I write the name of their organization. Then I ask the participants who the organization "knows." They come up with groups of people like volunteers, board members, donors, clients, vendors, etc.

After they understand the exercise, I ask them to do the same thing with themselves in the middle. Who do *they* know?

Use the same exercise when you meet to create your friendraising list with your staff and board members. When they've finished, have them think of one person from each circle who has potential inclination and capacity.

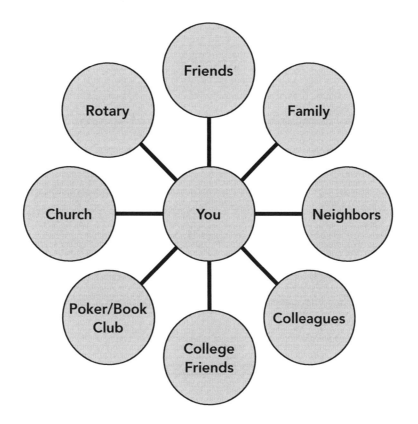

Not everyone they know will be philanthropically minded and interested in your particular cause (inclination), for example, or have the funds to make donations (capacity). With these facts in mind, ask your participants to select the one person from each circle (one friend, one family member, one neighbor, one colleague, one college friend, etc.) they believe is most likely to have both the inclination and capacity to give to add to your prospect list. You will need to cultivate these individuals more than you would if they were already donors to your cause, but you'll still have the advantage of starting with people you have relationships with through your board and staff members.

Fundraising is about relationships. By building on your staff and board members' existing relationships (their circle of contacts), you are much more likely to have success than by starting with strangers.

To Recap

◆ Your donor database is the best place to find prospective major gifts donors.

◆ Identify your largest and most loyal donors to include on your prospect list.

◆ Narrow your list down to the top twenty prospective major gifts donors.

◆ If you don't have a donor history, start with board and staff members' contacts.

Chapter Seven

Researching Your Prospects: The Fine Line between Professional and Creepy

IN THIS CHAPTER

···→ The ethical implications of donor and prospect research

···→ What do you need to know about your major gift prospects?

···→ How to do donor research when you don't have a dedicated researcher—the Internet is your friend

···→ The best research tool, bar none: ask!

···→ Crossing the line from research to creepy

···→ From "suspect" to prospect

To successfully solicit major gifts, you want to have as much information as possible about your prospective donors—without crossing the line, of course. Your research will tell you how much you can ask for, the types of programs your prospect is most likely to give to, and whether or not the time is right for the ask (after all, approaching donors right after their stocks have crashed isn't the best idea). The question: How much research is too much? (When does your research cross the line into "creepy stalker," and how do you stay on the "safe" side of the line?)

The Ethical Implications of Donor and Prospect Research

The Association of Fundraising Professionals (AFP) Code of Ethics requires members to "value the privacy, freedom of choice, and interests of all those affected by [our] actions." With that in mind, rest assured that the donor research I recommend is completely in keeping with AFP's standards.

Why? Because almost everything you initially need to know about a prospect is readily available on the Internet, without violating the prospect's privacy.

How does this work? First, remember that you're researching either people who are already your large or loyal donors or people your board and senior staff have identified during your initial friendraising meeting. This means you already know some key facts about them: their mailing address, for example, and/or what they do for a living.

Starting with these key facts, you can learn things like the value of a prospect's home, approximately (and sometimes exactly) how much a prospect earns yearly, and whether or not a prospect has made major contributions to other organizations.

As I've said, this is all publicly available information, and most or all of it is available for free. In fact, some very large nonprofit organizations are already well into using prospects' Facebook pages, Twitter feeds, LinkedIn profiles, and blog posts, among other things, to paint very complex and complete pictures of the individuals they want to approach for money.

Given all the information out there, then, how do you still "value the privacy" of your prospects and donors? By keeping everything you learn about them, public or private, in confidence. Never discuss the details of a donor or prospect beyond the boundaries of those in your organization with a need to know—for example, the board member you're sending to a major gift meeting with a particular donor.

> As discussed in earlier sections, it's important to keep donor information in your database, but don't put anything in a record that you wouldn't want the donors themselves to see. Remember, donors have the right to ask for their records at any time.
>
> You also want to have a confidentiality policy at your organization to protect the privacy of your donors.

Note: If you don't already, it's important that you create a confidentiality policy at your organization that says how your donor data will be used, who will have access, what is included in the records, etc.

What Do You Need to Know about Your Major Gift Prospects?

As I've mentioned, it's important to know as much as you can about a prospect before reaching out to ask for a major gift. However, given time and staff constraints at your organization, I don't want you to stress too much about donor research. As you'll see later in this chapter, the best way to research a donor is by asking the donor personally and not by doing a lot of formal research.

Here is a short list of the kind of information you need to know:

◆ Does your prospect have a high enough income or net worth to make a major gift?

◆ What kinds of assets does your prospect own?

◆ Is your prospect philanthropically minded?

◆ Is there anything in your prospect's background that indicates a potential interest in your organization or in one or more of your specific programs? For example, has the prospect lost someone to cancer, or did the prospective overcome poverty or hardship to rise to the top of his or her profession?

Some of this information is easily accessible via the Internet, and other information will need to come from the donors themselves.

How to Do Donor Research When You Don't Have a Dedicated Researcher: The Internet Is Your Friend

The only organizations I know of that have dedicated researchers on staff are universities. Occasionally, hospitals or big national organizations may have them too. However, if you're reading this book, it's highly unlikely that you have a dedicated researcher on staff.

But, as I mentioned in the section about ethics, most of the initial information you need to know about your prospects is publicly available—and free—via the Internet.

It's as simple as starting with Google. Just enter your prospect's name and state of residence as a Google search and see what comes up. If your prospect is well known in your area, you should find everything you need in the first results that come up. If not, you may need to scroll through a page or two. If your prospect has just received a large promotion or made a major gift to another organization, for example, there may be a news story online, or you may find the information via the employer's or organization's website or blog.

However, just as you want to follow the 90/10 rule when it comes to whittling down your prospects, you need to follow the same rule when doing prospect research online. Anyone who has spent any time on the Internet—in other words, pretty much everyone—knows how easy it is to get lost in the tidal wave of available information. You have only five hours per week, so don't spend very much time here.

With that in mind, here are four free online tools to help you target your online prospect research:

◆ Google: Don't spend more than ten minutes per prospect here. Do a quick search, make a note of any relevant news stories you find and the facts of those stories (which you can frequently find in the headlines and first paragraphs), and move on.

◆ LinkedIn (linkedin.com): This social networking site for professionals can tell you about your prospect's current job title (if you don't know it), job history, and business connections—including connections to the spouses or partners of your senior staff and/or board members.

◆ Zillow.com: Do you know your prospect's home address? Zillow can tell you the value of homes in that area and, thus, give you an idea of what your prospect's home is worth.

Spend some time doing basic research on the top twenty donors and prospects you identified on your prospect list.

◆ Salary.com: Plug in the person's occupation and the area where they live, and salary.com will give you the range of what people who share that occupation and location are making.

These sites will give you a good head start on your research. Getting the rest is up to your conversations with prospects.

The Best Research Method, Bar None: Ask!

Yes, the Internet is a quick, easy, and frequently free way to get started on prospect research. That said, in all my years of fundraising, I've found only one single 100 percent foolproof method to find out about other people—their likes, their dislikes, and whether or not they're willing to give.

That method? Ask! All the research in the world can't replace what donors will tell you themselves.

Granted, getting to know donors well is a process, and I will get into significantly more detail about it in the chapter on cultivation. In the meantime, here are some good initial "research" questions you can ask any donor or prospect (and not only will you be doing the best possible research, but you'll also be building a relationship when you take the time to ask your donors about themselves):

◆ Is philanthropy important to you? How do you demonstrate that in your life? (Do you volunteer or give to other causes?)

◆ What drew you to our charity/organization/cause in the first place? What made you decide to give the first time, and what makes you continue to give?

◆ What would inspire you to give more?

◆ How is your work going? How are your kids doing? What does your spouse do for a living?

◆ What do you do for fun/vacation?

These questions will give you some of the same information you can get while sitting in front of a computer. Does the prospect own a beach house in Costa Rica and go there with the family every year? If so, the donor obviously has disposable income to spend—and to give. Are your prospect's children in a private school? Is the family living on a single or dual income? All of these are important considerations when evaluating whether or not your prospect is able and willing to make a major gift. As an added bonus, you'll be able to get even more information by paying attention to your prospect's tone of voice and body language when you ask in person.

In addition, keep in mind that you can use the power of social media to continue and deepen your relationship and understanding of your donors. If you don't already have at least a Facebook account for professional purposes, start one today. Then be sure to submit "friend" requests to your donors who are also on Facebook. Some will connect and some will not, but it's a step in the right direction.

Finally, make sure that you keep your board members and senior staff involved in the donor research process. During your initial prospect or friendraising meeting, you learned, among other things, which members of your board and senior staff already know at least a few of your donors and/or prospects. Don't let the information gathering stop there. Check in regularly for news about the prospects they know, and encourage them to come to you as well.

> One time I was working at a university, and I had a ten-page printout from the research department about an alum I was meeting with later that day. I was feeling pretty good about myself, being armed with so much personal information about the person I was going to see. However, once I started chatting with the person, I soon discovered that my information was all wrong. Everything I had was about a different person with the same name!
>
> So, no matter how well you think you did researching someone, there's no replacement for asking the person directly. And it's a great reason not to spend too much time on research anyway—especially in a small shop, where time and resources are extremely limited.

 stories from the real world

Crossing the Line from Research to Creepy

When does donor research cross the line into being creepy? How much is too much information? This is something we all struggle with in the Internet age. Here's a simple test: Remember that donors have the right to request and view your files on them at any time. So ask yourself: Would they approve of the information you've gathered about them?

Avoiding coming across as creepy extends well beyond the information you seek out and keep in your donors' files. Imagine, for example, how you would feel if you were in a meeting and someone blurted out something like, "Bummer about that pay cut/stock portfolio/ little scandal involving your husband/wife/partner…" *That's* creepy! Why would you know that about your prospects unless they told you? You don't want your donors knowing you've done research on them.

This doesn't mean that you aren't ever allowed to discuss something you've learned about donors with them. If your prospect has just won an award and that information was covered

---

Suspects versus *Prospects*

A *suspect* is someone on your prospective donor list who is not necessarily familiar with your organization yet and/or may not have the financial resources to make a major gift.

A *prospect* is someone who has been identified as a prospective major donor for good reasons (at least a moderate amount of capacity and inclination).

We're not differentiating between the two for the purposes of this book, but it's important for you to know that in more sophisticated development operations, there is a difference.

---

by the media, by all means send a note or pick up the phone to express your congratulations! Likewise, it's always appropriate to send a sympathy or get-well card when you hear through the usual social or business channels that a donor has experienced a death in the family or an illness.

From "Suspect" to Prospect

In the major gifts world, a "suspect" is someone you think might be a good prospect, but you don't have the research to back it up. At least some of the people who start out on your "A" list, and many on your "B" list, may well be suspects in the beginning—particularly if you have put together a tentative list with your board during a friendraising meeting. Once you know a person is interested in your organization and has the means to make a major gift, that person becomes a prospect. While you may not need to differentiate between suspects and prospects in your small fundraising shop (particularly at first), this is a good technical term to be familiar with, since all the large development shops (like universities) use it.

To Recap

◆ Research plays an important role in major gifts work. It tells you who to ask, how much to ask for, what to ask for, and when.

◆ Donor research can be done ethically. Remember that everything you learn is confidential and should be shared only on a need-to-know basis.

◆ There are several free, labor-saving tools on the Internet you can use to do at least your initial prospect research.

◆ While an Internet search is a great initial step, the best research you can do is talk to individuals and ask questions to get to know them better.

◆ With limited time and resources, it is necessary to do only basic research on your prospective donors.

Chapter Eight

The Art and Science of Getting a Meeting: How to Meet with People You Know—and with People You Don't

IN THIS CHAPTER

···→ Understanding the goal of the first meeting

···→ How to get a first meeting with someone who doesn't want to meet

···→ Where to meet and who should attend

···→ How to meet donors from out of town

···→ How to let go of a donor who just won't meet

Many novice fundraisers try to hide behind mail, email, and their desks when fundraising. But this doesn't work, because fundraising is all about relationships, and you can't build a relationship without spending time with someone. Experienced fundraisers know that the best way to raise money is to be front and center with your donors. If you're going to build meaningful relationships with donors and raise even more money, you need to meet with them! After all, how often have you had a meaningful relationship with someone you've never met?

That said, some of your donors may live too far away to make frequent face-to-face meetings practical. But that's no excuse for anyone who has a computer and access to the Internet!

To raise major gifts, you will need to meet with all your prospects in person (or via video chat, when necessary). This includes people you already have a good relationship with (board members and volunteers) and people you'll be meeting in person for the first time.

Getting to Know You: the Goal of Your First Meeting

Whether or not you already know the prospective donor will determine the specific content of your first meeting. However, regardless of the content of your discussion, the goal of the first meeting is to strengthen the relationship and move toward a major gift.

Major gift fundraising is about trust. Would you give your money to someone you didn't trust? Probably not! Therefore, it's your job to build that trust with your potential donors.

Meeting with an Acquaintance

Before you can successfully ask for a major gift, you need to understand what makes your prospect "tick," how important philanthropy is to your prospect's life, and what motivates your prospect to give. To put it another way, this meeting is a logical extension of the donor research I talked about in **Chapter Six**. If you already have a superficial relationship with your prospect (you've seen the person at events, for example), you can get to know your prospect better by asking the kind of open-ended questions I mentioned in **Chapter Six**, such as:

◆ Why are you involved with this organization?

◆ What motivated you to give in the first place? What makes you continue to give?

◆ What other charities do you give to? Why are they important to you?

◆ What role does philanthropy play in your life?

◆ What would you like to see our organization do better/more of?

◆ What concerns you about our organization?

These open-ended questions will help you learn more about your donors and understand more about their motivations for giving.

Meeting with a Stranger

When you're meeting someone for the first time, your goal is to initiate a relationship that goes deeper than mail or email. Maybe this person has responded to your snail or email solicitations. That's a great start, but the relationship with your organization is superficial at best. The point of your first meeting with a new person, then, is to strengthen the relationship by getting to know the prospect and letting the prospect get to know you.

Start the conversation with something simple:

◆ Tell me about yourself. Where are you from?

◆ What do you (or did you) do for a living?

◆ Where did you go to school?

◆ What do you do to relax?

◆ What's your family background?

◆ Are you involved in other charities?

Remember that relationships are a two-way street! You'll want to share a little something about yourself in order to be relatable. But remember, this is a professional relationship, and you're not there to talk about yourself. Keep comments about yourself to a minimum while also participating in the conversation.

With that in mind, you will definitely want to share anything that you have in common, especially as it relates to your organization—such as cancer in the family, a history with alcohol, etc.

Meeting Someone You Know Well

When meeting with people you know well, like board members, you'll still want to ask questions to learn even more. You may already know, for example, how long someone has been on the board and why the individual originally joined. In that case, you could ask something like, "What's the one thing about our work that excites you most?" You can also ask if there's anything you can do to help make the job as board member easier. In addition to strengthening your relationship, you may learn some valuable tips for improving your board members' overall experience.

You may have noticed that I have mostly discussed focusing on the donor in the initial meeting and haven't mentioned talking about your organization at all. That's because most fundraisers err on the side of talking about their charities too much. Instead of focusing on your organization and what you do, focus on the donors and find out what's most important to them.

First Meeting Topics to Cover

In addition to asking whatever "getting to know you" questions are most appropriate, here are the most important points to cover in your first meeting:

◆ *Say thank you.* Most of the people you will be meeting with have given something in the past. Be sure to thank them for that support and let them know what was done with their contributions. Even if you've already done this, it's good to provide a reminder.

This is one key to getting another gift because it shows your donors that their contributions have gone to a good cause and because expressing your gratitude makes them feel adequately thanked and valued. Express gratitude for whatever they've done in the past, no matter how small, including taking the time to meet with you now.

◆ *Provide information.* Briefly cover the basics of anything your donor doesn't already know about your organization. Focus on any new programs or successes. Feel free to include any challenges your organization is facing, especially if the donor might have ideas or the ability to solve the problem with funding. But remember that while it's important to take some time to educate donors your organization, they can just as easily read this information online, in your newsletter, or in an annual report. Keep this part of the meeting brief—ten minutes or less—unless the donor continues to ask questions. Beware of boring your donor with too much detail or too many facts. If your donor's eyes start to glaze over, you know it's time to turn the conversation back to the donor!

◆ *Ask for advice.* Asking advice of your donors, no matter how well you know them, is a key feature of a successful meeting. If done correctly, there is no better way to engage donors and make them feel valued.

Ask donors you're meeting how they learned about your organization and if they have suggestions to help you do a better job. Ask how the organization is perceived in the community and how they think you might attract new supporters. Ask what they know about your programs and services and what they think should be improved.

Agenda for a First Meeting

◆ Thank your donor for previous support.

◆ Ask relationship-building questions.

◆ Briefly educate and update your prospect about your organization.

◆ Ask advice about your organization.

◆ Invite prospect to get involved as a volunteer.

◆ Move toward a gift—schedule a follow-up tour, meeting, or other activity.

A final word on your first meeting: Lend donors your ear (and be sparing with your words).

What's the number-one thing people love talking about? Themselves, of course! So be sure the meeting is focused on them!

You may know the popular expression "you were given two ears and one mouth for a reason," so use both appropriately. Listen twice as much as you talk, and let donors talk about themselves—their favorite topic!

How to Secure a Meeting

Now that you know the purpose of the meeting and what to say once you get there, I'm going to backtrack and talk about how to get the meeting in the first place.

Sometimes picking up the phone to schedule a meeting can be the hardest (scariest) part. Many development directors prefer to send "precall" letters, especially if they don't know their prospective donors, to introduce themselves and let donors know that they will call to schedule an appointment. These days, you can send a letter of introduction via postal mail or email. But no matter how (or even if) you send a letter beforehand, you still need to pick up the phone to schedule your appointment.

Of course, picking up the phone is just the beginning. As you may know from experience, many people will resist meeting in person. They'll have a variety of excuses why they can't or shouldn't meet, and you need to be prepared to overcome all of them in a thoughtful (but not a pushy) way. You'll hear these excuses from strangers, acquaintances, and even donors you already know well.

No matter how people dress them up, their objections to meeting generally come down to two basic ideas:

> ◆ I'm too busy. I don't have time to meet in person.

> ◆ I don't want to be asked for money.

Your job is to come up with counterarguments (without being argumentative).

Addressing the "I'm Too Busy" Issue

Let the person know that you really want to meet in person but that you will be brief and the meeting will last only fifteen minutes. Then stick to that timeframe. At your meeting, when you're approaching the fifteen-minute mark, ask if the donor has a few more minutes. If the meeting is going well, the donor will usually say yes, but you must be respectful and end the meeting if the donor says no.

Addressing the "I Don't Want to Be Asked for Money" Issue

Assure the donor that you won't be asking for money at this meeting. Say you'd like to thank the donor (in person) for past support and to ask for advice. Be clear that you would like to start a conversation about support in the future but that you will not be asking for money at this time.

Remember, your goal is to get a meeting. You're highly unlikely to get a major gift if the prospect won't even meet! That said, how many responses can you come up with to rebut these rejections?

As I said a moment ago, even donors you know well may resist meeting in person. In fact, it may actually be even more difficult to get a meeting with your board members than with strangers! Why? Because your board members may think they see you all the time—when, in reality, you have never seen them in a non-group setting. Do you really know how they feel about your organization? How do they feel about serving on your board? It's just as important to meet with your board member major gift prospects as it is with prospects you've never met before.

However, don't worry about it if you have donors on your list who just won't meet. Thank them for their time and consideration. It's unlikely that they'll be ready to make a major gift in the near future, so move them from your list of "A" prospects to your "B" list. More on this at the end of this chapter.

Board Member Connections: Key to Opening Tough Doors

If you're having trouble getting a commitment to meet with a prospect who is connected to one or more of your board members, don't hesitate to use those connections. Ask your board members to help you connect and set up meetings with the people they've referred to you. Even if a member can't or won't attend a meeting personally, having the member call to ask the person to meet with you will help tremendously.

> Take some time to secure meetings with your top five major gift prospects. Use whatever method necessary—write a precall letter, pick up the phone, or send an email. Before you call, identify and prepare for any objections your prospects may have. Write down your responses so you can address each objection even if you get flustered while on the phone.

Choosing a Location: Where to Meet

The best place for a one-on-one meeting is at the individual prospect's home or office. The meeting doesn't need to take place in a restaurant for a meal, or even at your office. In fact, there is really only one hard and fast rule about meeting location: Hold it wherever it will be most convenient for your prospect or donor. The only caveat to this rule is to try to hold your meeting in a quiet, interruption-free space where you can have a meaningful conversation.

The idea that prospects should be taken out for a meal is a common misperception. Remember, you want your meeting to be relaxing and free of interruptions; a difficult thing to achieve in almost any restaurant. Other complications over meeting at a restaurant include where to go, how to talk and eat at the same time, and concerns about who pays. All these issues can be avoided by meeting at the prospect's home or office.

Who Should Attend?

Ideally, your organization should be represented by two people at the donor meeting: the executive director and director of development, a board member and the executive director, or some other combination. Executive directors should be reserved for meetings with *big* major gifts prospects, and other staff members can meet with lower-level prospects. Board members should go whenever possible, especially if they have existing relationships with prospects.

What Should You Bring?

You don't need to bring anything. Sending follow-up materials is a great excuse to stay in contact, and it's easier to keep the conversation light and distraction-free if you leave the paperwork at your office. If you're more comfortable bringing facts and figures, bring them. But don't pull them out unless specifically asked.

However, if you have a great video—particularly a moving first-person story from someone your organization has helped—and you have a computer with a large enough screen and the capacity to play it, this is exactly the kind of "prop" you can use to open up your conversation with the donor. However, the video should be less than five minutes long. If it's longer, give the prospect a copy to for viewing later.

After You Meet: Your Follow-Up Plan

Never leave a major gift meeting, even a first one, without first establishing a follow-up plan for what's going to happen next. Each meeting should get you one step closer to asking for that major gift, and the follow-up plan is critical to making that happen.

If you feel the meeting went well and you're ready to make the ask, your follow-up plan can go something like this:

"I'm so glad we had the opportunity to meet today. I value your thoughts about our organization and will consider them carefully (if you asked for advice). I'd like to send you some additional information (if appropriate) as we discussed, and I'd like to schedule another time, in about a month, to come back and talk with you about how you can support us in a more significant way. Would you be open to that type of conversation?"

If you're meeting with someone for the first time, a more appropriate follow-up plan might look something like this:

"I'm so glad we had the opportunity to meet today. Is there any additional information I can send you? Would you like more information about volunteer opportunities? Will you come for a tour?" (Don't ask all of these. Select just one or two appropriate questions to make sure you'll have another meeting and/or cultivation opportunity.)

Long-Distance Meetings

It's highly likely that at least some of your donors won't be a short drive away. What do you do when you have a prospect who lives far away? Since nothing replaces a face-to-face meeting, you need be creative and do your best to get in front of your long-distance prospects. Ask if your prospect has any plans to be in your area in the next month, or even somewhere between the prospect's location and your own. Offer to meet them at the prospect's convenience during any travels. Remind the prospect of this periodically. You don't want to miss meeting when your donor comes to town.

Of course, it might be worthwhile to go all the way to the prospect depending on the level of gift you're considering asking for. Is a $10,000 gift worth a plane ticket and one night in a hotel? Probably. If you're really fortunate, there will be additional donors in the same area and you can have more than one meeting during the trip.

If all else fails, use technology to your advantage. Most people know how to video chat these days. Even seniors chat with their kids and grandkids, so don't assume your older prospects don't have or don't know how to use online technology.

Long-distance donors can be a challenge, but continue the conversation the best you can over the distance and do your best to get together when your schedules allow. Don't let distance come between your organization and a potential five, six, or even seven-figure donation!

How to Let Go of a Donor Who Just Won't Meet

As we discussed earlier, no matter what you do and how well you do it, the fact remains that some people on your list just won't be willing to meet with you. Don't give up on these people completely, but do move them to your "B" list and continue to gently and periodically cultivate them. The fact is that they're unlikely to make major gifts if they won't make meetings, but you never know…

And I *do* mean that you never know. One of the readers who's been following the Major Gifts Challenge on my blog wrote in to say he finally got a meeting with a prospect after cultivating that person for three years!

In other words, persistence can pay. However, be smart and don't waste your time either. Stay open to meeting and try once a year, but don't cross the line to becoming a pest.

To Recap

◆ The goal of your first meeting is to move one step closer to a major gift. This means getting to know the donor, listening more than talking, and making sure to have a follow-up plan before the meeting ends.

◆ Be prepared for objections to scheduling a meeting. Use tools like a precall letter or email to ensure you get a meeting.

◆ Meet in a quiet, private spot, like the prospective donor's home or office. Bring a board or higher-ranking staff member when appropriate.

◆ You can create and maintain relationships with long-distance donors by scheduling meetings when they're in town, going out of your way to visit them, and using technology to keep the relationship going over the miles.

◆ Some people just won't meet. When that's the case, they're unlikely to make major gifts anyway. Don't stress. Move on to the next prospect on your list.

Chapter Nine

How to Build Deeper Relationships with Major Gift Prospects

IN THIS CHAPTER

---> The importance of cultivation in getting major gifts

---> Who can participate in relationship building, and how?

---> How to create a cultivation plan for each prospect

Would you give a large amount of your hard-earned money to someone you've just met? If you're like most people, you just answered that question with an emphatic "No way!"

Well, if you wouldn't give significant money to a stranger, why would you expect a prospect to give you a major gift before getting to know and trust you and your organization?

This is a truth that bears repeating (which is why I've mentioned it several times): It takes trust and strong relationships to raise major gifts. Your first meeting with donors begins that process. However, that's just the first step. To successfully raise major gifts, it's necessary to build relationships between donors and key leaders at your organization—primarily your executive director and members of your board of directors. That's what this chapter is all about.

I also want to make it very clear that cultivation isn't just for major gift donors. We'll talk about donor acquisition and retention later in the book. What needs to be mentioned here, though, is that the steps you take to properly cultivate *all* your donors now will save you even more time and effort in acquiring new donors later.

What Is Cultivation?

The second stage in the fundraising cycle is called cultivation. Just like you build a beautiful garden by cultivating the plants, you also build a strong bottom line by cultivating—building relationships with—prospective major donors. Cultivation is the essential step between identifying prospective donors and making the all-important ask. Remember, your success or failure in raising major gifts hinges on how well you know your donors!

Just like your first meeting, the goal of each cultivation activity is to move you one step closer to asking for—and receiving—a major gift. Therefore, here are the key questions you need to ask yourself before and after each cultivation activity:

Before the Activity

How will this (meeting, tour, event, etc.) bring me closer to asking for a gift?

After the Activity

◆ What did I learn about the donor, and how will that help me secure a gift?

◆ Did I learn, or learn more about, what motivates the donor to be philanthropic?

◆ Did I find out what the prospect loves most about my organization and which area(s) the prospect would like to see grow?

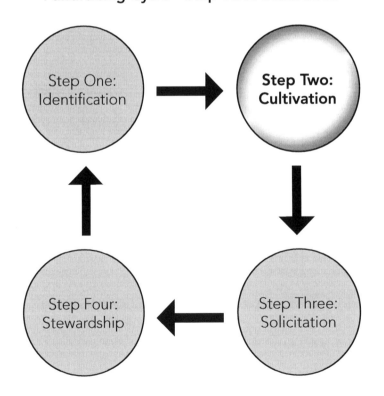

Fundraising Cycle—Step Two: Cultivation

To put it another way, cultivation is the ongoing process by which you get to know your donors, and they get to know you, on a deeper level. Cultivation involves routine and regular contact with individual prospects, educating them about your organization, and building a sense of trust and engagement. A successful cultivation process gives you deep insight into what your donors are passionate about—and the things that inspire them to give.

I touched on this in the last chapter, but I can't stress enough that cultivation—most of all—is about listening. One of the most common mistakes made by executive directors, development directors, and board members is that they're so eager to share the story of their organizations that they forget to listen. Listening to and hearing the person you're cultivating is the most important part of the process!

So how do you cultivate a successful donor relationship—one that leads to major gifts? It starts with the in-person meeting I focused on in the last chapter. From there, there are many ways to build relationships.

When we stop to think about it, cultivation isn't really that complicated. Think about the ways you maintain relationships with your friends and family. You get together and visit; you go out socially; and you email, call, and text one another. You provide updates and information and sometimes ask for advice. All of the above are also things we do in cultivation.

Since the primary goal of cultivation is to get to know your prospects better, you'll want to continue to ask the kinds of open-ended questions we started out with in the last chapter:

◆ How did they get involved with your organization originally?

◆ Why did they decide to start giving, and why do they continue to give?

◆ Why do they feel your mission is important?

◆ What do they love about your organization, and what would they like to see improved?

◆ If they could fix or improve one thing about your community or the world, what would it be?

> Think about cultivation just as you would think about maintaining and building relationships with friends and family: You get together, go out socially, call to check in, text, email, ask advice, etc.
>
>

These questions encourage donors to think about your organization on a deeper level—and to dream about how they can make the world a better place.

Staff versus Board Roles in Cultivation

Board and staff members each have an important role to play in building relationships with prospective donors. Board members will want to help with cultivation, particularly if they will participate in asking prospects for major gifts. After all, it doesn't make sense to have a board member appear for an ask meeting if the member has never met the donor before.

If possible, assign to each board member on your major gifts committee, as well as any others who are willing to help, two to three major gifts prospects to help cultivate throughout the year. Give the board members a list of specific responsibilities—for example, sitting with "their" prospects at events, bringing them on tours, signing letters to them, calling them with updates, etc.

While it's the job of your board to help the process, staff members are the people who are ultimately responsible for implementing the cultivation plan and keeping it on track.

Cultivation Activities

There are many ways to cultivate, or build, relationships with people.

In-Person Meetings

Meeting with someone face to face is the number-one type of cultivation activity, and it should appear on every one of your prospective donors' cultivation plans. Face-to-face meetings are the only type of situation where you can truly get to know your donor on a more personal level.

Tours

Taking someone on a tour of your organization is another great way for you to get to know the person—and for someone to see your programs and services in action. Don't leave this tour experience up to chance! Donor tours should be well thought out, planned, and even scripted. If appropriate, set up a chance for the prospect to chat with a happy client. Make sure your executive director is on hand and available for a quick five-minute meeting somewhere along the tour.

However, tours aren't the right cultivation tool for every kind of organization. If most or all of your work takes place in an office setting, that's hardly the kind of environment to inspire a major gift from a donor. If the nature of your organization prevents you from creating exciting in-person tours, either create a virtual tour with pictures, testimonials, a video, etc., or skip this activity altogether.

Volunteer Opportunities

One of the best ways to cultivate donors is to engage them with your organization, and there is no better way to engage and feel ownership of an organization than by volunteering with it. If you can persuade a prospect to volunteer over a period of time, it will be much easier to successfully solicit a major gift from that person. Volunteer opportunities come in all shapes and sizes. Could the prospect serve on a committee? Provide service directly? Help in the office? Engage the other employees at his or her company for a special cleanup or other day of service?

Small-Group Events

Cocktail parties or dessert receptions are popular cultivation activities at many organizations, but I have to admit I'm wary of them because I've seen them done badly more often than not.

On the one hand, small get-togethers (like a cocktail party at a board member's home) are great for attracting new potential supporters to your cause and an effective way to make it easy for board members to make introductions to their friends. The problem lies in the follow-up. If you don't follow up immediately with the guests who attended, you may as well not have held the event at all. Make sure to put a follow-up plan in place before hosting small-group events.

Phone Calls

A quick phone call is a great way to build a relationship. Call with a quick, but important, update. Call to thank someone for a gift. Call to invite a donor to a program or event. These calls will let your prospective donors know that you're thinking of them. More importantly, these kinds of calls are ways you can do something for your donors, not just ask them what they can do for you.

Correspondence

Writing is quickly becoming a lost art, so if you send your prospective donor an actual handwritten note, it won't soon be forgotten. It's always nice to send a card when a donor is sick or for a birthday. Or add a personal note to an article or newsletter when you mail a prospect. And, while it's less personal, email also works to communicate with your donor. The point here is that it's important not to be a stranger between visits.

Creating a Cultivation Plan

Returning to the garden metaphor for a moment: Just as you wouldn't treat every one of your plants the same, it's very important to have an individual cultivation plan for each major donor on your list.

Here are the four simple steps to building a plan. You can do them in any order that makes sense.

Face-to-Face Meeting

This is a must. You cannot discuss a major gift in a group setting!

See Your Organization in Action

Invite all your prospects to take a tour, visit a program, or attend an event.

Engage

Invite your prospects to volunteer. Volunteering brings people closer to your organization and makes them more inclined to give.

Provide Updates

Updates about your programs and services can be delivered by phone, by email, in person, or by handwritten note. Updates should be delivered approximately twice annually to all prospects on your list.

Sample Cultivation Plan

Name: Sue Jones

Month	Activity	Responsible Party	Deadline/ Status	Notes
January				
February	Invite on a tour	Board member		
March				
April	Invite to gala	Development director		
May	Email with program update	Development director		
June	Invite for face-to-face meeting	Executive director		
July				
August	Invite to volunteer	Development director		
September	Handwritten note update	Executive director		
October	Solicitation meeting	Executive director/board member		
November				
December	Holiday card	Executive director		

Notes: _____

_____

_____

_____

_____

Create a simple one-page cultivation plan that works for each of the twenty prospective donors on your list.

Sample Cultivation Plan

Prospective donor name: _____

Assigned volunteer: _____

Month	Activity	Responsible Party	Status
January			
February			
March			
April			
May			
June			
July			
August			
September			
October			
November			
December			

Solicitation (ask) meeting date:_____

Amount to ask for:_____

Notes: _____

_____

_____

_____

_____

_____

_____

_____

If all the components of your plan are basically the same, why have a different plan for each donor? This is where your donors' individual likes, dislikes, and preferences come into play. One donor may love one-on-one meetings but feel shy and uncomfortable in larger group settings. You obviously don't expect this donor to attend your annual dinner of over one hundred guests. Likewise, some of your major donors will prefer email updates, while others will prefer phone calls. Not only that, but different prospective donors will also require a different degrees of cultivation depending on their existing relationships with the organization. Board members have already been cultivated and may need only one meeting before deciding to make major gifts. Others you may be meeting for the first time will need significantly greater amounts of cultivation.

Create Cultivation Plans for Prospects on Your List

Develop a cultivation plan for your top twenty prospective major gift donors, customizing each one based on the individual's needs and preferences.

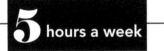

Getting to know and respecting your donors' preferences in this way is a key component to building the necessary trust to ask for a major gift.

Long-Distance Cultivation

As I discussed in the previous chapter, sometimes your donors don't live nearby. Regardless of the distance, though, you still need to cultivate them just like you do the donors who live close to home! Be creative in your use of technology with such donors if they're open to doing so. Send a few more notes than you do to the donors you see more often—and include photos from selected events to help them feel more connected. And, of course, try to make plans to visit when they're in town or travel to meet them if and when appropriate.

Building relationships takes time. Depending on who you are cultivating, it will take more or less time. Board member prospects have already been cultivated for years. Donors you are meeting for the first time will take more time to build meaningful relationships.

To Recap

◆ Cultivation is the second step in the fundraising cycle and is the process to building deeper relationships with your prospective donors.

◆ There are many ways to build relationships with donors. The best are in-person meetings, tours of your organization, and engaging donors in volunteer activities.

◆ It's important to create an individualized cultivation plan for each prospective donor on your list.

Part Three

The Moment of Truth: Asking and Beyond

Part Three covers what to do leading up to the ask, how to ask, and how to ensure you get major gifts again and again. While you may be tempted to skip directly to Part Three, try to restrain yourself. Each part builds on the others, and you won't be nearly as successful with major gifts if you skip directly to Part Three. However, once you get to Part Three, you will learn who should attend the ask meeting, how much to ask for, and more. You will also learn the best language to use to make the ask as well as what to do if you get a *yes*, *no*, or *maybe* response from your donor. Part Three concludes with how to thank and follow up with your donors.

Chapter Ten

Get Ready to Ask

IN THIS CHAPTER

···→ The who, what, when, where, and why, of asking

···→ How to schedule the ask meeting

···→ Who should make the ask and how

···→ How much should you ask for?

The ask—the moment a fundraiser sits down with a donor and directly asks for a gift—is the part of fundraising that ties many people's stomachs in knots. If the thought of fundraising makes you feel ill, this is almost certainly the piece that has you scared. After all, telling your organization's story and being friendly come fairly easy to most people who work in nonprofits.

That said, unless you ask, you won't raise money. It's not that easy (for many), but it is that simple.

Scheduling the Ask Meeting

If you've done a good job with cultivation and built a solid relationship with your prospect, you shouldn't have a problem calling or emailing to set up the ask meeting.

But, of course, this phone call or email is different from the ones you've sent to invite the prospect to events or for a tour of your organization. When you reach out to the donor this time, it's important to be honest and fully explain the purpose of the meeting. The prospect should understand that you want to discuss financial support of your organization. The last thing you want to do when asking for a major gift is to catch your donor by surprise. Think about it. How likely would you be to make a major gift—or any gift—if the request caught *you* completely off guard?

By being upfront about the purpose of this meeting, you're not just letting the prospect know what to expect—you're also laying the groundwork for your ask. After all, if the prospect says yes to an ask meeting, that's a great sign that the prospect is at least ready to think about making a gift and wants to hear what you have to say.

Timing—When Should You Schedule the Ask Meeting?

The sooner you ask for a gift, the sooner you're likely to receive one. Your organization needs the money, so don't hesitate or procrastinate. And, remember, this is for your annual fund, so you will want to ask once a year. That means your cultivation can't stretch longer than one year. Trust the expression "there's no time like the present."

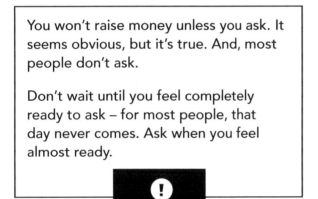

You won't raise money unless you ask. It seems obvious, but it's true. And, most people don't ask.

Don't wait until you feel completely ready to ask – for most people, that day never comes. Ask when you feel almost ready.

! important

Of course, you don't ask for a major gift during your first meeting (as we discussed in **Chapter Eight**), but after that, trust your gut.

You should ask for a gift once you feel reasonably ready—after you've done your research, had your first meeting, and gotten to know your prospect well enough to have an idea of which things about your organization interest and excite your prospect the most.

My rule of thumb is that once you've been through several of your cultivation activities—in other words, you've had an in-person meeting, given a tour, and possibly attended one event with the prospect—you're ready to ask.

The one caveat here is that before you set up the ask meeting, you need to have had at least one conversation with your prospect about the needs of your organization and the impact of the donations you've received. If you've failed to raise the issue of money in your face-to-face cultivation meeting, you run the risk of catching your prospect by surprise with your ask—which, as I said, is never a good thing in major gift fundraising.

Where to Ask?

As discussed earlier, restaurants aren't good places for serious meetings in general—and they're *definitely* not the place you want to meet when it's time to ask for a gift! There are so many things that could go wrong in a restaurant, including noise level, inability to talk and eat at the same time, a waiter interrupting at exactly the wrong minute, and the awkwardness of who pays the bill.

Asking for a major gift is a sensitive, serious, and confidential conversation. Why would you have that conversation in a public place?

The best place to ask for a gift is the same as the best place of your initial meeting—wherever the prospect feels most comfortable. This is often at the donor's home or office. If you've already met in one or both of these locations, you'll be more comfortable there as well.

It's also good to note that when donors invite you into their home, it's highly likely that they will make some level of gift. It's unlikely that they would want to engage with you on such a personal level if they didn't truly care about your organization.

Who Should Attend the Meeting?

Determining who should attend an ask meeting can be like putting together the pieces of an intricate jigsaw puzzle, except in this scenario there are lots of combinations that can work.

> When I was a new fundraiser, I learned the hard way about where not to ask. Of course, like so many new fundraising professionals, I took a prospective donor to a restaurant to make the ask. I was feeling pretty good, because lunch went well and we were having a great conversation. I was planning to ask over coffee and dessert—at the end of the meal. Unfortunately, the individual said she didn't have time for coffee and ran out as soon as the meal was over!
>
> **stories from the real world**

Spouse/Partner

When scheduling your ask meeting, be sure to ask if the prospective donor's spouse or significant other should attend. Giving, especially when it comes to major gifts, is generally a family decision, and not one that one spouse or partner makes without consulting the other. It's even better to have spouses or partners present if you've already included them in the cultivation process.

Also, don't assume that the family's breadwinner makes the philanthropic decisions. In fact, in most households, women play a larger role in making the donation decisions—even in cases where the husbands earn most of the money.

Obviously, it's up to the donors who attends from their side, but it's always better to be inclusive when you schedule the meeting.

From the Organization

It's always nice to have two people from your organization attend an ask meeting whenever possible. Ideally, send your executive director and a board member who has a relationship with the prospective donor.

Never take someone the donor hasn't met. After all, this is about relationships!

Executive Director

As I've discussed previously, it's very important that your executive director be an integral part of the major gifts process. This includes attending ask meetings. Your executive director is your organization's visionary—the person your donors need to know and trust to do good things with their contributions.

Board Members

As I mentioned above, you should always include a board member who has a relationship with your prospect, who is one of your prospect's peers, and who has been involved in cultivating the prospect. Not only that, but ideally this board member is the person who should be tasked with making the ask. If the particular board member who qualifies in these other respects is unable or unwilling to make the ask, this person should still be present if at all possible.

Why a member of the board and not the executive director or director of development? Remember, your board members hold a unique position as people who are giving of both their money and their time. Board members are volunteers, and their income won't be affected in any way by a prospect's decision to make a gift—as opposed to staff members, who rely on donations for their salaries. In fundraising, perceptions are as important as relationships!

In addition, have you heard the expression "peer-to-peer fundraising"? This refers to people being more receptive to being asked when the asker is someone they can relate to, generally because they're in the same social or professional circles or the same socioeconomic class. Most nonprofit staff members aren't in the same "class," for lack of a better word, as potential major donors. As you know, very few nonprofits can afford to pay the kinds of salaries that make it possible for staff to make major gifts themselves! The prospective donor and board member, on the other hand, are "peers," or equals, on a variety of levels, which makes the board member the ideal person to ask for a major gift.

Finally, and most importantly, the board members or other volunteers you send to major gift meetings must have made their own gifts first. They need to be able to say they've "put their money where their mouth is" before they ask anyone else to do the same. It's okay if the board member you send to the ask meeting isn't a complete social or financial "equal" with the prospect, as long as the asker has made a significant (significant for the board member, that is) gift.

Board members who are familiar with your prospective donors are ideal askers—but they have to make their own gifts first before they can ask anyone else to do so!

If you don't have the "right" people to make the ask, then you're on your own. Don't wait for the perfect combination of people to make the ask. You may be waiting forever. As Nike says: "Just do it."

Development Staff Members

Again, if you've done your job as outlined in **Part One** of creating a culture of philanthropy in your organization, you should seldom need to send a member of the development staff to attend ask meetings. However, if you start the process of ask meetings while still developing your board, or if something prevents your executive director and/or a member of the board from attending an ask meeting, the responsibility falls to the development director or development staff. After all, it's your job to raise money, and the job needs to get done.

Of course, it could also be the case that the development director or other staff member is the person who recommended and introduced the prospect to your organization in the first place. If that's the case, by all means include that staff member in the ask meeting!

As you can see, there are many combinations of people who can be sent to your major gift ask meetings. Ideally, it's the executive director and a board member. However, there are plenty of times when the executive director and development director are teamed up—or the development director can go with a board member.

And, in many organizations, it just doesn't work to have two people attend. In that case, you're on your own. It's more important to ask than to wait for the "right" combination of people.

What Should You Ask For?

When you ask for a major gift, it's vitally important to ask for the money to meet a specific need, even if that specific need is unrestricted funds. Major donors want to know where their money is going and are much more likely to give if you ask them for something specific.

Based on your cultivation conversations, you should have a good idea of your donors' areas of interest. How do they feel about funding unrestricted operations? Are they interested in specific programs or services you provide? Do they want to see you grow in a particular area? Will they provide salary support?

Yes, major donors like to know where their money is going, and they like to be asked to fill specific needs. But what if your specific need is funds to pay salaries and other bills so you can keep your programs going? If that's the case, then during cultivation, you should have discussed the importance of operations with your prospects to determine whether they're open to the idea of supporting operations.

Here's where rubber meets the road in major gifts fundraising. Asking for and getting a major gift is about the ability to tap into your donor's deepest passions to support something the donor can't refuse. What type of gift will make the donor feel wonderful? That's exactly the gift what you need to ask for!

Determining the Right Amount—How Much Should You Ask For?

Now that you know what you'll be asking your prospect to fund (or help fund), it's time to determine how much money you'll ask the prospect to give. This is the part of the ask that all development and executive directors struggle with the most.

Unfortunately, there is no exact formula for determining how much to ask for, but I'll give you a place to start: You're going to ask for between two and ten times the amount the prospect has given *annually* in the past. You may or may not want to include what the donor has given in terms of ticket purchases, etc. That's up to you.

For example, if your prospect has given $1,000 annually and also attends your gala or other yearly event, your starting point will be an ask of from $2,000 to $10,000 (two to ten times the annual gift amount).

That's quite a range, isn't it? But don't worry. Now we're going to narrow it down a bit more.

Next, consider the entire giving history of the individual. Has the prospect just given once— say, last year—or for many years? In other words, are how committed is this person to your organization?

Has the donor made increasingly bigger gifts over the years, or has the gift size remained the same?

Remember, in **Part Two**, we worked on researching your donors. Now it's time to use that research. In addition to giving history, what do you know about your donor? Where does your donor work? What does the spouse or partner do for a living? Is your donor retired, single, or supporting kids in college? What type of home does the prospect have? What types of cars? Does your donor have a vacation home or take lavish vacations? Where else does the donor give, and how much? Consult all the data you've gathered on this prospect. Once you've answered as many questions as you can, it's almost time to decide on the amount you will ask for.

> Donors don't want to give to a sinking ship, so don't seem desperate. Come at the ask from a position of strength. Explain how you're the only organization doing what you're doing (or in the specific ways you're doing it or in your geographic region) and why the need is so great.
>
> Motivate donors by tapping into their passion and letting them know how they can help.

The last factor is your organization's needs. Donors are moved and motivated by the needs of the organization. That's not to say that your donor will be able to give you everything you need, but your prospect might give more than otherwise planned if you articulately explain what your organization needs and why.

Also, no donor wants to save a sinking ship, so don't act desperate. Instead, present the need from a position of strength—for example, yours is the only organization in the area that feeds the hungry, and you need additional resources to do that.

Using the above combination of factors, decide on an ask amount—and then double that number. Yes, double it. Why? Because if you've never asked for a major gift before, it's likely that you're uncomfortable doing so and, thus, will be inclined to ask for too little. Therefore, if at first you decide to ask for $2,000, I suggest doubling that and asking for $4,000. The donor may surprise you and give you exactly what you ask for!

Of course, it's also possible that you may not get the first amount you ask for, so start high and negotiate down. It's okay if the donors tell you they can't give what you're asking. Use the ask as a starting place. The prospects will let you know what they can do.

So here's the formula for coming up with an ask amount:

1. Figure out what a donor has given annually in the past. Your starting place will be anywhere from two to ten times that amount.

2. Factor in assets, occupation, lifestyle, etc., to determine if you will ask at the high or low end of that range.

3. Determine what you need, and use that as a factor as well.

For example:

Jane Doe gives $1,000 annually. So you will ask her for between $2,000 and $10,000. You know she lives in a big house, has a high-powered job, doesn't have any dependents, and is very philanthropic. Therefore, you will ask at the high end. It turns out that you need $9,500 for a specific program or service that Jane is interested in. Therefore, you will ask Jane for $9,500.

The most important thing to understand, however, is that you must ask for a specific amount. Asking someone to support your after-school program without saying how much you need only leaves a donor confused. At that point, if you get a check for $100, the donor has done what you asked—even if you were hoping for $1,000. Donors aren't mind readers. You've got to tell them what you want.

Scheduling the Meeting

Now that you've decided who, what, when, where, why, and how much, it's time to set the meeting. Whether you initiate the meeting by phone or email (depending on how the donor likes to be communicated with), it's time to schedule a meeting.

> You must ask for a specific amount. If you ask for program support without asking for a specific amount, you'll confuse your donor and it's unlikely you'll get the amount you're hoping for!
>
>

Be sure to let the donor know why you want to meet. Don't be coy. Say you want to meet to discuss how the donor can get more involved and be supportive in a more meaningful way.

As I've said, you don't want to surprise your donors. They should know exactly what the meetings are about. This enables them to think about their gifts in advance and allows you to have productive conversations. If donors aren't ready to make gifts of any size, it's unlikely they will agree to meetings.

All that being said, don't allow yourself to get sucked into asking over the phone (unless distance is an issue). Let donors know that you really want to discuss this in person so you can both give the topic your full attention. However, if time is an issue, feel free to commit to a twenty-minute meeting if that's what it takes to get the donor to agree to meet.

Getting Ready to Ask—Role-Play

You've determined what you're going to ask the donor to fund and how much money you'll be asking for. You've chosen the people who will represent your organization at the ask meeting. Now it's time to rehearse the actual ask.

Get Ready to Ask

◆ Identify a prospect you're ready to ask.

◆ Determine the who, what, when, why, where, and how much of your ask.

◆ Schedule an ask meeting with the prospect to be solicited.

◆ Role-play (practice roles with the people going to the ask meeting).

5 hours a week

You may think you've already taken care of the preparation. After all, you've researched and cultivated this prospect. You've decided what your organization needs and how much you're ready to ask for. Isn't that enough?

No. In fact, absolutely not!

Preparing for the actual ask is a part of the process that will ensure you're completely prepared. You'd never give any other kind of business presentation without first practicing it, right? Well, think about an ask meeting as any other type of presentation, because that's what it is. Not only that, but it's a presentation where your goal is to motivate your audience to do something big.

First, assign roles and responsibilities for the meeting. If you're going with your board member or the executive director, who will do what?

I mean this literally: What role will each person serve in the meeting?

> ◆ Who will open the meeting with small talk?
>
> ◆ Who will recap your relationship, expressing gratitude for the prospect's past giving?
>
> ◆ Who will provide a quick update about your current programs or services?
>
> ◆ Who will actually ask for the donation—and how?
>
> ◆ Who's responsible for making sure you don't leave the meeting without a follow-up plan?

Each person at the meeting needs specific roles and responsibilities, and you should role-play them before the actual ask meeting. (I'll go into more details about this and more in the next chapter, so keep reading.)

To Recap

◆ Once you've done sufficient cultivation, it's time to schedule the ask meeting. And be up front about why you want the donor's time.

◆ Select your asking team carefully, and be sure to include your prospect's spouse or partner in the meeting invitation. The people who attend the meeting from your organization should have the closest relationship with the prospective donor.

◆ Use the prospect's giving history and the research you've completed in **Part Two** to decide your ask amount.

◆ Be specific in terms of what you're asking for and how much!

◆ Assign roles for the ask meeting and practice them before you get there.

Chapter Eleven

The Moment of Truth (Time to Ask)

IN THIS CHAPTER

- ---→ Ask meeting basics (what to bring)

- ---→ The meeting agenda

- ---→ How to ask (ask language)

- ---→ The importance of being quiet

- ---→ How to respond to the three donor responses: *yes*, *no*, and (my personal favorite) *maybe*

I like to call the ask meeting "the moment of truth." This is the moment you've been building toward from the day you started with your donor database and determining your organization's major gift levels back during **Part One** of this book.

But even though this is the moment of truth—the meeting where you plan to ask for a major gift—it's important to remember that although *technically* you're asking for money, you're not *actually* asking for money. Instead, you're asking your prospects to support your organization's vision, mission, and important work. If you keep this in mind, the ask itself will be easier.

In addition, remember that although you may be very attached to your organization, your donor's response to the ask isn't personal, and you shouldn't take it that way. How an individual gives away money is personal to the donor—not to you. So do your best to keep your emotions out of it. If you don't get a particular gift, you have to believe that you're one step closer to the person who will make a gift—just like in sales.

Fundraising Cycle—Step Three: Solicitation

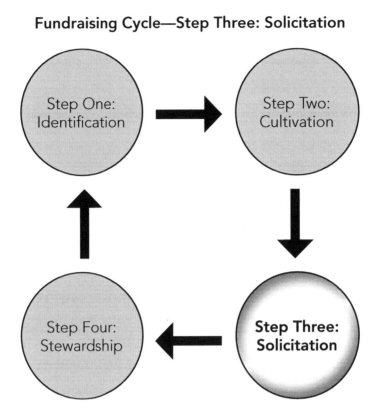

For some (many) people, the ask meeting and actual ask are the most intimidating parts of the major gift process. For others, the first cultivation visit is actually more difficult. But whether the butterflies started flitting about your stomach the first time you met with the donor or now, as you're ready to make your ask, this fact remains: You won't get a major gift unless you ask for it.

Now let's dive in and talk specifics about how to make that major gift happen.

So, you arrive at the prospective donor's home or office at exactly the appointed meeting time. (Arrive early and wait down the block in your car so you are right on time.) If you didn't carpool with your asking partner, wait for your partner before knocking on the donor's door. Now what?

Ask Meeting Basics

Before we go to the next step, let's take a moment to review the items you should have with you when you're standing at your donor's door. Much of what I'm about to say may sound completely obvious while you're sitting here calmly reading this book, but you might be surprised how easy it is to lose track of vital details when you're getting ready to leave for an ask meeting—particularly if this is your first one! With that in mind, here's a list of the basics that you should have in hand when you arrive:

◆ Your organization's major gift packet, including whatever written materials you've created and your business card. (There's a good chance you've already presented this material during the cultivation stage—in which case, you won't need it.)

◆ Your laptop if you planning on showing the donor a video. Make sure your battery is charged beforehand. Don't count on the donor having an outlet that's convenient to where you'll be sitting during your meeting. (Again, if you've already shown your video during cultivation, you won't need this.)

◆ Pens and a notepad to jot down any questions the donor has that you don't have immediate answers for. There's little worse than forgetting to respond to a donor's questions promptly when you've just asked for a major gift!

The Meeting Agenda

While an ask meeting isn't a formal event like your board or other business meetings, there is a certain order, or agenda, that is part of every successful ask meeting. (Remember in **Chapter Ten** when we discussed assigning and practicing roles? This is where that piece of planning comes in handy.)

Here is your ask meeting agenda. Before you show up at your donor's door, you and your asking partner should know which one of you will handle each item—and ideally (as I said in the last chapter), you should have practiced together at least once.

1. *Small talk.* This is just what it sounds like: asking how the prospect has been since you last met and basic catching up. Generally, this should take only three to five minutes.

2. *Recap.* Next, it's time for five minutes worth of recap. Remind the person why you're there, thank the donor for past support, and briefly discuss your organization's vision for the future.

3. *Ask.* The moment of truth has finally arrived. In one or two sentences, ask for the gift. Yes, that's right. Just one or two sentences. Why? Because if you've done your cultivation correctly, you've already set the stage for the ask. The donor knows your organization and knows you. Repeating everything you've already told your prospect during the ask is not only unnecessary, but it can also be irritating!

4. *Silence.* For many people, this is the hardest part of the ask. It's also crucially important. You've told the prospect what you want. Now it's the donor's turn to talk and respond to your request. (I'll talk more about this in a moment.)

5. *Follow up.* Be prepared to follow up on your donor's response and answer any questions.

That's it. An ask meeting can take as little as fifteen minutes if there's not a lot of small talk, updating, or recapping to do. Of course, it can also take much longer, so don't rush things if your prospect isn't in a hurry or has lots of questions.

How to Ask (Ask Language)

The one question I get asked the most about face-to-face fundraising is "How do you actually ask someone for money?"

Why is this such a difficult subject? For one thing, as we discussed in **Chapter One**, our culture has a taboo around talking about money (though this is changing). Many people in our culture consider asking how much other people make for a living to be as personal a question as asking about their sex lives—if not more so! In addition, asking someone else for a monetary gift opens us up to potential rejection. And nothing makes people nervous than the idea of being rejected, even if the rejection has nothing to do with them personally.

And, of course, there's still that taboo around asking for money in the first place. Put all this together, and it's no wonder that so many nonprofit professionals and volunteers need coaching on how exactly to phrase the ask!

With that in mind, below is a sampling of ask language for you to try. Practice these requests in the mirror until you feel more comfortable. And, of course, adjust the language to fit your organization, goal(s), and donor(s):

> When asking for a gift, you can ask for a gift "in the range of" X amount of dollars but not give an actual range.
>
> Why? Because asking for a donation "in the range of" gives the donor the chance to name a different amount rather than just say yes or no. In addition, if you actually give a range—say, $1,000 to $5,000—donors will almost always choose the lower amount in the figure even if they would have otherwise given more.

practical tip

Board Member to Prospect

"Mary, you've been such a great supporter of this organization, and we want to thank you again for that. As you know, we need more funding to accomplish the XYZ goals that we have been discussing. I've given what I can, and I'm here today to ask you to join me and to consider a gift in the range of $5,000 to support our after-school program."

Executive Director to Prospect

"Mary, as you know, we are so appreciative of all the support you've given us over the years. Thank you again for being a partner in our mission and for enabling me and the rest of the staff to carry out this important work. I'm here today to ask you to consider a gift this year in the range of $5,000 to support our after-school program to allow the children we serve to continue to have a safe and welcoming place to go after school."

When asking, *always* include a specific amount to support a specific program or service. (Even if that specific "thing" is unrestricted operating funds. If that's the case, ask the donor to support the overall work of your organization.)

The Importance of Being Quiet

Once you've gotten the ask out of your mouth, the hard work is about to begin.

Why? Because (as I said above) once you've made the ask, it's time to be quiet and give the prospect a chance to respond.

Think about it. If you're squirming in your seat with sweat pouring down your brow while you're waiting for your donor to respond, and you just can't wait any longer... If you speak first, you'll start backpedaling the moment you open your mouth.

What do I mean by that? If you ask your prospect for $5,000 and there's an awkward pause... If you can't keep your mouth closed, the only possible thing you can say will be, "I know that's a lot—how about $1,000 instead?" If you talk first, you *will* ask for less. There's nothing else to say or do.

With this in mind, you may want to practice being quiet after your ask every bit as often as you practice the ask itself. Once the ask is out of your mouth, you have put the ball in your prospect's court. Your one and *only* job now is to be quiet until the donor responds.

> Once you've made the ask, be quiet, no matter how awkward or long the silence may seem. The ball is in the donor's court. It's the donor's turn to speak next.
>
> If you speak first, the only thing you can do is backpedal by asking for less.

important

How to Respond to the Three Donor Responses: *Yes, No,* and (My Personal Favorite) *Maybe*

There are three possible answers, and only three, that a person can give after being asked for a major gift: *yes, no,* and *maybe.* Therefore, you need to be prepared for all of them.

Let's say you ask someone for a major gift and the response is:

> When you get a major gift—celebrate! Order pizza for the office for lunch, or have a dance party in the hall. Whatever you do, remember to celebrate each and every major gift you receive, and make it fun!
>
> In addition, take a moment to remind yourself why you're doing this work in the first place—by taking a few minutes to review the good your organization has done in the past and will do as the result of this gift. These breaks and reminders make the hard work of raising major gifts more fun.

important

◆ *Yes.* Thank the donor, of course! Next, find out how your donor would like to make the gift. Will the donor write a check? Should you send an envelope? Arrange a time to pick it up? Does the donor wish to pay by credit card? By giving stock? *Don't leave the meeting until the "when" and "how" are determined, or you could be in the awkward position of having to ask again or needing to remind the donor.*

After you leave, be sure to follow up as promised. In addition, send a thank-you letter with a personal note the same (or the next) day. (Note: This thank-you letter is not the same as the tax-receipt thank-you letter, which cannot be sent until the gift actually arrives.) A thank-you call from someone who attended the meeting is also in order when someone makes a major gift.

Finally, make a note that you probably asked for too little and to ask for more next year. After all, the donor was able to say "yes" right away, and didn't need to think about it for long—a sure sign that you could have gotten more!

◆ *Maybe.* Maybe is actually my favorite answer. Why? A *maybe* means you asked for so much that the person needs to think about it, but not so much that the response was an immediate *no*. Great job—you hit the sweet spot!

When a person needs to think about it, or says maybe, you must have a response ready. For example, ask good questions like:

❑ Can I get you more information to help you make your decision?

❑ Do you have any questions that I have left unanswered?

Once again, don't leave the meeting without a follow-up plan. Ask when you can follow up to find out if the prospect has made a decision. Once you agree on a date and time in the near future (should be one to two weeks), it's your job to follow up. If you don't, it's as if you never asked in the first place. The donor will *not* follow up with you.

What If I Ask for Too Much?

If you ask for too much, don't worry. The donor will be sure to tell you! If this happens, you have a few options. One is to ask what amount might work better for the donor. Another is to ask if the donor would like to give that amount but spread the gift out over a period of months or years.

Always be appreciative regardless of how much the prospect ultimately gives. Although you may be disappointed if the gift is smaller than you had hoped, think of this as the beginning. If you are truly grateful and you continue to do a good job cultivating your donor, a first gift could end up being the first of many that will ultimately add up to more than you had asked for originally!

◆ *No.* What do you do when a person you've just asked for a major gift says no?

Believe it or not, *no* is frequently just the beginning. I once heard one of my fundraising mentors say that "the best fundraiser is the one who can turn a *no* into a *yes*."

Why is it possible to turn a *no* into a *yes*? Because in fundraising, there are actually two kinds of *no*: the *hard no* and the *soft no*.

A *hard no* means "not now, not ever." The good news, if you've done your cultivation correctly, is that you should never hear this variety of *no*.

So let's assume you get a *soft no*. This kind of *no* can actually mean a variety of things:

❖ Bad timing. ("You didn't know, but I just got laid off from my job/my spouse has fallen ill/my investments have just taken a bad turn," for example.)

❖ Wrong amount (you asked for too much or too little).

❖ Wrong project (you asked for the wrong thing).

Or it could mean a variety of other things. In order to turn that *soft no* into a *yes*, then the first step is to find out exactly what the *soft no* means. To do this, be prepared with open-ended questions and turn the conversation back around to the person being asked.

After getting a *soft no*, say something like:

"I'm sorry to hear that. I thought you were interested in supporting the program (project) in a bigger way. Can you tell me a bit more about how you want to help or what you were considering?"

Or:

"I'm sorry to hear that. Were you thinking of a different amount, or is there a way I can work with you to help make a gift in the range of *X* amount possible for you?"

Your job is to keep the conversation going and the dialogue open. Ask if the prospect needs more information, time, or something else. If you don't end up converting the *no* into a *yes* at this meeting, tell the donor you hope you can continue the conversation.

Regardless of your prospect's ultimate response, be gracious and truly grateful. Thank the donor for taking the time to meet with you and for all the support for your organization to date.

> Plan to meet with at least one prospect to make the ask this month. Practice, plan, make the ask, and follow up.
>
>  hours a week

Then make a follow-up plan to revisit the issue (unless the prospect needs to get more engaged first—in which case, extend an invitation to attend an event and/or to volunteer again).

After your meeting, regardless of the outcome, send a thank-you note!

To Recap

◆ The ask meeting is your "moment of truth," so be prepared in advance with a practiced agenda and everything you'll need for the meeting.

◆ Prepare your ask ahead of time—and then be prepared to be silent and let your prospect respond.

◆ Be prepared for yes, no, and maybe.

◆ Be truly grateful, and send a thank-you note (not the tax-receipt thank-you letter) after any meeting, regardless of the outcome.

Chapter Twelve

More Than Simply *Thank You*

IN THIS CHAPTER

 ---→ What gratitude really means

 ---→ How and when to thank your donors

 ---→ How to create a stewardship plan

 ---→ The importance of telling donors how their gifts were used

Our parents taught us the importance of saying thank you, but why do these words matter so much? Because of the sentiment behind them. What we're really talking about here is gratitude. In the context of fundraising, are you truly grateful for what your donors do? What about when they give us less than we were hoping for? How can we be truly grateful for whatever our donors do for our organization, and how do we express that gratitude?

As the final of the four stages of fundraising, stewardship (or gratitude and follow-up) is equally as important as the first three. Sadly, this is often the step that is shortchanged, as people are so eager to move on to the next step.

Why Is Gratitude Important?

Two of the key reasons that donors cite for not making second gifts to organizations:

1. They weren't thanked properly.

2. They weren't told how their first gift was used.

Fundraising Cycle—Step Four: Stewardship

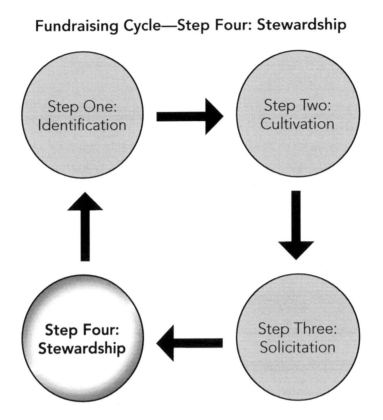

Remember, the major gift process doesn't end with receiving the gift. In some ways, it *starts* there. But if you think of your donors as human ATMs—you go to them only when you need some cash—you'll find that they're quickly closed for business.

After all, why do donors give? They give because giving feels good. And part of your job is to make sure they feel great about giving to your organization.

"What Do You Think?" (Value Your Donors' Opinions)

If you want to raise truly major (huge) gifts, you need to value and respond to your donors' opinions, including listening to their needs and desires when it comes to their philanthropic donations. Donors give because it feels good and because they want to do good—and major gift donors give because they want to do good in specific ways. By listening to your donors' opinions and responding to their feelings about the good they want to do in the world, you don't just make them happy. You also assure them that their money is being put to uses that fit their vision—in other words, that their money is being well spent.

In addition to assuring donors and figuring out the best way to match their philanthropic desires with your organization's mission, the fact is that most major donors have the money to give because they are accomplished individuals. Soliciting your donors' opinions may well help your organization do its work even better!

As you begin thinking about major gifts, take some time to think about what your donors do for your organization. They don't simply give money. They save lives. They feed the hungry and house the homeless. They educate children. They help cure diseases. They make sure beaches are cleaned, rain forests are preserved, and abandoned pets find homes.

Donors are so much more than simply people who give money to your organization—and until you start treating them that way, they'll have no real incentive to give you a penny more.

Creating a Stewardship Plan

So right now, before you take the next step toward raising major gifts, it's time to create your stewardship plan. How will you thank your donors so that they understand the impact they've made on your organization? How will you make them feel so appreciated that they'll want to give over and over again?

Sadly, I've come across too many organizations where donors aren't thanked at all. Staff and board members believe thanks are unnecessary, and then they wonder why they struggle with fundraising! Do you think *you* would give a second time to an organization that didn't thank you for your first gift?

Ask yourself: Do you have the technology and administrative support to have a multipronged approach, or do you have the capacity for only a one-size-fits-all approach? The more customized and personalized you can make your letters, the more success you will have.

Think about the following when creating your stewardship plan:

◆ Can you send different letters to first-time donors versus repeat donors? If possible, send first-time donors "welcome" thank-you letters.

◆ Repeat donors should be acknowledged as loyal donors. Let them know that you know they're loyal donors.

◆ How will major gifts donors be acknowledged differently from other annual fund donors?

◆ What role will board members play? Will they sign thank-you letters? Will they make thank-you calls?

◆ What role with the executive director play? Will the executive director sign all thank-you letters? Is that a good use of the executive director's time?

◆ What level of donors will get a personalized note and/or a phone call? Only major donors? All donors?

◆ What roll will the development and administrative support team play?

In general, donors give two reasons for not making second gifts:

◆ They were not thanked.

◆ They were not told how their money was used.

Do not let either of these excuses be valid for your donors.

In addition to thanking your donors in multiple ways by multiple people, be sure to let them know how their gifts were used. Approximately six to eight months a the gift is made (and at least one month prior to asking for another gift), be sure to let your donor know how the gift was used.

For major gifts (and major donors), you will want to let them know in person. Schedule meetings with donors to let them know how their gifts were used, and then reiterate it in writing via thank-you notes. You could say something like, "We want you to know how meaningful your last gift was to the children we serve. Your generous support enabled us (in part) to provide an additional teacher in the resource room after school. As a result, kids' grades have been going up. This would not have been possible without your donation."

For smaller donors, you could say something similar, but in an email or letter (as opposed to in person). Although they probably didn't fund something fully, you want to emphasize that their donations, in combination with those of others, really made a difference.

The Rule of Seven Thank-Yous

The rule of thumb is that you should thank a person seven times before asking for another major gift. "Really?" you may be thinking. Yes, I know that seems like a lot of thank-yous, but you want to make certain that your donors feel your gratitude before you ask for more. And, yes, you can thank donors repeatedly without becoming a pest or sounding fake. You don't need to limit your expressions of gratitude to the ones you say or send directly to the donor.

Here's a sample schedule for the seven thank-yous:

1. Thank the donor at the ask meeting.

2. Have a board member or the executive director (if one attended the meeting) call to say thank you after the meeting.

Create a Stewardship Plan for Your Organization

Set aside time to determine who, when, and how you will follow up with your major donors. A good rule of thumb is that each donor should be thanked in multiple ways by multiple people. This could be by phone, in person, by email, by being listed in your newsletter, etc.

In addition, you need to tell donors how their gifts were used before you ask for more.

Individual donors have different preferences as to how they want to be thanked, so a key part of your stewardship plan will be to ask all donors how they would like to be recognized, thanked, and communicated with.

Write two or three thank-you letter templates, which can be customized as you receive gifts. Different letters should be used for first-time donors, repeat donors, long-time donors, etc.

Finally, if your organization doesn't already have a stewardship plan for *all* your donors, this is the time to create one. Thanking smaller donors properly is one of the first steps to moving them up the ladder to giving more!

 hours a week

3. Write and send a thank-you card as a follow-up to the ask meeting.

4. Send a tax-receipt thank-you letter within forty-eight hours of receiving the gift.

5. List the donor in your annual report, on your website, and/or in your newsletter (get permission first, of course).

6. If appropriate, list your donor on a donor wall and/or thank the donor publicly at a special event.

7. Follow up six to eight months after the gift was made to let the donor know how you spent or are spending the gift. (While you're doing this, it doesn't hurt to add another thank-you!) This update can be in person, by phone, or by email.

And, of course, express your gratitude for the last gift immediately prior to asking for another one.

Whew! That was a lot of gratitude! But it's well worth the effort, because repeatedly demonstrating your gratitude significantly increases your chances of receiving another, even larger, gift!

Saying Thank You at the Ask Meeting

Regardless of whether a person says yes, no, or maybe when I ask for a gift, I *always* respond with "thank you." Yes, even when prospects say no, I still thank them for their time and consideration—and you should too.

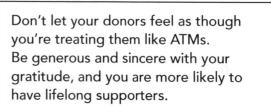

Don't let your donors feel as though you're treating them like ATMs. Be generous and sincere with your gratitude, and you are more likely to have lifelong supporters.

important

Thank donors for their engagement and involvement. Thank them for taking the time to meet with you. Thank them for listening to your proposal and considering your request— unless, of course, you want this meeting to be your last.

Think about it. You and/or your board took the time to identify, research, and cultivate these donors because they have the potential to give the kinds of gifts that will help your organization thrive and grow. In return, the donors have already given to your organization, even if they've given "only" their time. By being gracious and grateful at every step of the process, you are assuring your prospect that your organization has both class and integrity.

After the Ask

As I mentioned above, there are several opportunities to say thank you after the ask meeting where you've received a gift. We'll elaborate on the different ways to say thank you throughout the rest of the chapter, but remember this important principle we discussed in **Chapter One**:

Have multiple people thank donors at multiple times and in multiple ways. This way, your donors aren't receiving all the thanks from the same person or in the same format. In other words, it's obvious that your entire organization is aware of and appreciates what they've done.

Be sure to tailor your expressions of gratitude to your donors' preferences. Some donors love getting a call from a board member, others are more touched by a personal note, and still others love seeing their name in the annual report or newsletter. Regardless, make sure you've covered all your bases.

Not sure how your donors want to be thanked? Ask them!

Asking donors how they wish to be thanked is easy. You can say something like: "We'd like to show our appreciation for your generosity. Is it okay if we list you in our annual report and on our website?

And, for that matter, ask how they wish to be communicated with in general (and make a note of it). "Do you prefer communications by mail, email, phone? Do you have a strong preference?" Always do your best to communicate with your donors via their preferred method.

Written Gratitude

For tax reasons, it's important to send your donor a formal letter on your letterhead confirming the date and the amount donated. Your letter should state whether any goods or services were provided in exchange for the donation or if the donation is fully tax deductible to the extent of the law.

I once worked for an organization where the executive director wanted to handwrite notes on each and every thank-you letter. You may think this sounds like a great idea, but what actually happened was that the letters sat on his desk for weeks (and weeks) until he made time to add notes to all of them. And the bigger the donation, the longer it sat—while he waited for inspiration about the "perfect" note to write. Some of the biggest donors waited weeks (or months) to receive their thank-you letters. Instead of helping the process, he was hurting it—exactly the opposite of his intention!

stories from the real world

The best practice is to send this letter within forty-eight hours of receiving the gift, but in my experience, a one-week turnaround is standard for small shops. If it's taking your office more than one week to mail thank-you letters, you need to revamp your system—a topic I'll address a bit later in this chapter.

You may already have a generic tax receipt you send to donors, but don't use these for your major donors! Instead, add some extra oomph by personalizing them and stating what the donor's gift will be used for. If you absolutely have to use your generic form due to budgetary or time constraints, be sure to add even a few sentences on the letter so donors will know the letter is really just for them.

If you want to give your tax receipt letter some extra zing, add a handwritten, personal note on the side, top, or bottom of the letter. No space? No problem! Use a Post-it for your special note.

Is adding a personal note to your letters slowing you down? Send the initial letters right away, and then follow up with a written card later. In addition—regardless of whether you managed to add a note to the tax-receipt letter—it's also important to send handwritten thank-you cards to all of your major donors. Keep a stash of cards (and stamps!) in your desk for those occasions. They can be preprinted with your organization's logo, or they can even be plain stationery from a card store.

Saying Thank You Leads to More Gifts

A few years back, there was a major study done that measured the impact of a thank-you call from a board member. The study showed that if a board member called to say thank you within twenty-four hours of the organization receiving a gift, subsequent giving went up by over 37 percent. And the call worked even if the just caller left a message! Can you imagine an easier way for a board member to have a major impact on fundraising? I can't! So ask your board members to volunteer to make thank-you calls.

> ### Sample Thank-You Script for Board Members
>
> If you are going to have board members make thank-you calls—which I highly recommend—you'll need to make the job easy for them by providing a script. Here's an example:
>
> "Hi, my name is Sarah, and I'm a board member at XYZ organization. I'm calling to thank you for your recent generous gift. We really appreciate your support."
>
> That's it. There's no need for small talk or a longer conversation.
>
> However, board members should be prepared to answer questions or know where to refer donors if they do have questions that the board member can't answer.
>
>
> important

Of course, if a board member participates in the ask meeting or knows the donor, it should be that particular board member who makes the call. This is also a great way to involve your board members who can't or won't ask for gifts!

Giving Back to Donors—When Are Gifts Appropriate?

I had a development director call me once to say, "Help! My executive director is sending a fruit basket to *every* donor!" Just to clarify, I asked, "Every donor? Even to those who sent twenty-five dollars?" "Yes!" he said. Every. Single. Donor.

Yikes!

How do you think those donors felt when they received their fruit baskets? I know how I'd feel. I'd feel like the organization had wasted my money!

That said, gifts to donors are occasionally appropriate—especially for major donors—but they need to be considered thoughtfully and judiciously. How will your donor feel about receiving a gift?

Depending on the size of the donation, you may decide to give "tchotchkes" as tokens of your gratitude, but many donors don't even want those.

If you know your donors well, it might be appropriate to send the occasional "special something" or to present a donor with a plaque. However, over many years, I've learned that donors generally don't want or need anything other than your sincere gratitude. And, as we've discussed, that gratitude can be expressed in many ways.

Formal Ceremony

Organizations often recognize major donors at galas or other types of recognition ceremonies. At such ceremonies, it's appropriate to present donors with plaques or other types of inscribed gifts. This meaningful method of saying thank you is an experience that, if done well, will have a real impact on donors and their feelings about your organization.

Creating an Acknowledgment System

I mentioned above that if it's taking you longer than one week to get thank-you letters out the door, it's probably time to evaluate or re-create your acknowledgment system.

An acknowledgment system can be simple or complex, depending on the structure and staffing at your organization.

Here are the basics:

1. A check arrives in the mail or a credit card gift is received online as the result of your major gift ask.

2. A bookkeeper or similar staff person logs and deposits the gift and lets critical staff members know that a major gift (or a smaller gift from your core list of donors) has arrived.

3. Simultaneously, the donation is entered into your database.

4. A thank-you letter should be automatically generated.

5. Someone must personalize the autogenerated letter.

6. A live stamp (not postage meter) is added to the envelope.

7. Within one week of receiving the gift, the letter goes in the mail.

Make sure that key leaders at your organization are alerted to the arrival of any significant gifts so that they can make calls and send handwritten cards (if this has not already happened).

Stewardship Goes Beyond *Thank You*—Tell Donors How Their Gifts Are Used!

The last important part of the stewardship process is to follow up with your donor six to eight months after they make gifts to let them know how it's going. Why six to eight months? Because you'll be asking for another major gift a year out, and you don't want to wait to tell donors how you used their last gifts at the same time you're asking for more!

Sample Stewardship Plan—By Gift Size

Gift Size	Tax Letter—Development Director, Admin, or Volunteer	Handwritten Note—Executive Director	Phone Call—Solicitor (Person Who Asked) or Development Director	Follow Up (How the Gift Was Used)—Executive Director or Development Director
$1 to $199	Within one week			In eight months—letter
$200 to $499	Within one week			In eight months—letter
$500 to $999	Within forty-eight hours	Within one week	Within one week	In eight months—letter and phone call
$1,000 or more	Within forty-eight hours	Within one week	Within one week	In eight months—letter and in person

Sample Stewardship Plan

Fill in the blanks, and include who is responsible and in what timeframe.

Gift Size	Tax Letter	Handwritten Note	Phone Call	Follow Up (How the Gift Was Used)
$1 to $199				
$200 to $499				
$500 to $999				
$1,000 or more				

As I've mentioned, one of the main reasons donors cite for not making second gifts is that they weren't told how their previous gifts were used. Don't let this be an excuse, real or perceived, for your donors.

Create a stewardship plan that works for your organization. Your plan should outline in detail what will happen when gifts arrive, how and when the donors will be thanked, and how and when they will be informed how their gifts were used.

If you haven't told your donors how their gifts were used, or thanked them properly, pick up the phone today!

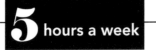

If any particular donor's gift wasn't enough by itself to fully fund any one thing, you can say something like, "Thanks to your gift and the donations of others, we were able to buy a van for the after-school program," or "We were able to pool your gift with other donations to hire an additional homework aide for our after-school program," or "Thanks to your generosity, we were able to continue our research into a cure for thyroid cancer."

Ideally, you want to tell donors in person how their gifts were used. This is more cultivation and propels you toward the next major gift. If you can't meet in person, tell donors in multiple ways at multiple times how their gifts were used. Send handwritten notes or emails, or even pick up the phone. Make sure they know how their gifts were used and how much it was appreciated.

Stewardship is an extremely important part of the fundraising process. Don't neglect it simply because it comes after the gift is made! That's one of the biggest mistakes you can make, because you will be alienating your biggest and best donors.

To Recap

◆ Create a stewardship plan.

◆ Use the "Rule of Seven Thank-Yous"

◆ Thank-yous should come multiple times, from multiple people, in multiple ways.

◆ Thank-you calls from board members make a sizable difference!

◆ Tell donors how their donations were used *well before* asking for more gifts.

Part Four

Taking Your Organization to the Next Level

Part Four is critical if you truly want to take your organization to the next level. There are many ways to take your organization to the next level, including conducting a capital campaign, starting to solicit planned gifts, and providing ongoing professional development for your key staff members (not to mention raising major gifts for the first time). You may or may not be ready for a capital campaign, but it's important to know why or why not. In Part Four, you'll learn that it's easier than you think to start accepting and soliciting planned gifts. Part Four concludes with the importance of donor retention and how to make sure your fundraising staff members are doing the best job they can by keeping up with the most current and best fundraising practices.

Chapter Thirteen

Considering a Capital Campaign?

IN THIS CHAPTER

···➤ What is a capital campaign, and how do annual and capital campaigns differ?

···➤ How do major gifts differ between capital and annual campaigns?

···➤ Why it's important to raise major gifts as part of your annual fund.

U p until now, this book has focused on major gifts in a noncampaign context. This is extremely unusual, because most nonprofit staff and board members who are unfamiliar with major gifts associate major gifts with capital campaigns. After all, most of the media coverage that takes place around fundraising is all about the capital campaign of the local hospital, school, or other charity, right? It's seldom that we hear much about particular gifts given to annual funds, so it's no surprise that you live with this as your reality.

That said, this book focuses on major gifts in the context of annual funds because I believe that nonprofits should raise major gifts regardless of whether or not they are in a campaign. Even more importantly, working on major gifts throughout the year is the perfect preparation for a capital campaign. After all, why would you expect to be able to raise the much larger gifts that are the focus of capital campaigns without first building your experience on the smaller, but still significant, major gift asks that should be part of your annual fund work?

Finally, I always advise my clients to start their major gift work with asks during their normal annual fund campaigns because it's the best way to supercharge their annual funds and raise significantly more revenue for programs and services. In addition, there's the added benefit of educating themselves about how to ask for major gifts. Another benefit is educated donors who have gotten into the habit of giving major gifts to your organization. In other words, raising major gifts in a non-capital-campaign environment will teach your staff and board members how to work together to ask for and give major gifts as well as prepare your donors to expect you to ask—and to ask for more and larger gifts in the future.

Think about this in the context of your own giving. Say you give $100 a year to your local animal shelter. If you were to receive a visit out of the blue from one of the shelter's board members asking you for a $10,000 gift to fund an expansion of the facility, how would you feel? Shocked? Possibly even offended? I know I would!

On the other hand, if you've grown used to being asked for—and to giving—an increasing amount over a number of years, that $10,000 ask isn't likely to be very surprising. If the shelter has cultivated you correctly, in fact, you'll probably thank the shelter for asking as you get out your checkbook.

Now that we've reviewed the reasons that you should start working on major gifts as part of your annual campaign well before your organization embarks on a capital campaign drive, let's talk about what a capital campaign is, what it's for, and how this kind of campaign—and the gifts that are given during such a campaign—differs from an annual campaign.

What Is a Capital Campaign, and How do Capital and Annual Campaigns Differ?

A capital campaign is a special, once-in-a-while type of campaign that organizations hold when they're looking to raise special funds for long-term needs. Capital campaigns are often used to raise money for things like new buildings or expansions of existing facilities. Universities use them to meet those needs and also to fund things like scholarships or new programs. A comprehensive capital campaign also often has an endowment fund component.

A good analogy to explain the difference between capital and annual campaigns is to compare them to your household budget. An annual campaign covers things like your grocery and electric bills and other day-to-day expenses. A capital campaigns covers long-term needs like a new roof—or even the down payment for your mortgage.

A *capital campaign* is a special, once-in-a-while type of effort that nonprofits undertake to raise significant monies to fund long term needs like new buildings, scholarships and endowment funds or to start new programs. Capital campaigns are designed to raise significantly more money than annual fund campaigns and are multiyear in nature.

Campaign Timing

Another difference between an annual fund drive and a capital campaign is the time commitment involved. As you know, your annual fund always takes place during a twelve-month period, whether that be the calendar year or your organization's fiscal year.

Capital campaigns, on the other hand, generally last much longer, with the average being between three and five years. The shortest capital campaign I've worked on, in fact, lasted three years—while my longest such campaign lasted seven.

Amounts Raised

Annual funds raise dollars needed for ongoing programs and services. This amount is closely related to your annual budget (although it may be only a fraction of your actual budget if you receive fees for services or other income).

A capital campaign, on the other hand, is designed to raise many times what you normally raise annually, and it should be taken very seriously.

Remember that a capital campaign doesn't replace your annual fund drive. In fact, you'll be holding both simultaneously. After all, you don't stop paying the light bill because you're putting money away for a new roof! The same holds true with annual and capital campaigns. You need to keep raising money for your ongoing needs even as you simultaneously solicit much larger gifts to finance long-term needs.

As I've said throughout this book, you can significantly improve your nonprofit's budget by spending just five hours a week on major gift fundraising for your annual fund. You need to commit significantly more time and resources to create a successful capital campaign!

How Do the Major Gifts Given in Capital versus Annual Campaigns Differ?

Although you will have an internal goal for your annual fund, you don't announce or celebrate it like you do the formal monetary goal in a capital campaign. For your annual fund, each donor will be approached individually for a major gift, generally for existing needs or an expansion of current programs and services.

When you're raising capital funds, be sure to ask each donor for a campaign gift *and* an annual gift simultaneously. This is called a double ask.

Let's say you have a donor who gives $1,000 each year to your annual fund. When you ask for a capital campaign gift, you may ask for a capital gift of $10,000, paid over five years ($2,000 per year), *and* for $1,000 per year for the normal annual gift—for a *total* gift of $15,000 over five years ($10,000 for the campaign and $1,000 per year during the course of the campaign to maintain your organization's regular programs and services).

In a capital campaign, on the other hand, you need leadership gift givers—people who pledge early to kick things off and motivate others to give. This really isn't the dynamic with the major gifts you solicit for your annual fund.

Another key difference between major gifts in a capital and an annual campaign lies in the way organizational leaders approach each type of campaign. Significantly more planning and resources go into a capital campaign than an annual campaign. Organizations often hire consultants and additional staff to help throughout a capital campaign. On the other hand, consultants are generally used in annual campaigns only for specific and shorter-term needs.

There are other differences between the gifts given during capital and annual campaigns as well. Capital campaign gifts are often pledged and paid over multiple years, as opposed to annual major fund gifts—which are, of course, given every year. (However, there are exceptions to every rule. Some donors may decide to give their entire capital gifts up front, for example, while an annual fund major donor may make a multiyear pledge.)

Another difference between capital campaign and annual drive major gifts is that capital campaign gifts often include more complex gift agreements, and are frequently made by giving assets—like stocks, life insurance, or real estate—instead of cash.

The size and complexity of the major gifts that nonprofits seek during capital campaigns is the main reason these kinds of campaigns are so time- and labor-intensive. It takes a lot of research and planning to raise money for a capital campaign while also maintaining your annual fund drive!

To Recap

◆ Capital campaigns are different from annual campaigns because of what they raise funds for. Annual fund campaigns raise funds for current operating and programmatic needs, whereas capital campaigns raise funds for long-term needs.

◆ Capital and annual campaigns also differ from one another in terms of the length of the campaigns and the size of the campaigns.

◆ You should begin raising major gifts as part of your annual fund so that you are prepared when the time comes to do a capital campaign.

Chapter Fourteen

Can a Small Shop Really Do Planned Giving?

IN THIS CHAPTER

- ···→ What is planned giving?

- ···→ Why it's important for your organization to ask for planned gifts

- ···→ "You want to give us what?" (the importance of strategic partners in planned giving)

- ···→ Avoiding trouble before it comes up (gifts policies)

Yes! You can be the beneficiary of planned gifts, no matter how small your organization or your staff. All you need is a mission that donors believe will be relevant for many years to come—and the capacity to work toward that mission.

While you need to have policies and procedures in place that define how and what types of planned gifts you'll accept, and what you will do with the money, you don't need any special staff or even expertise to accept them.

Why am I including a section on planned giving in a book about major gifts? Because in the past several decades (a process that's still going on), there has been and is a huge transfer of wealth happening between the generation of people who lived through World War II and their children, the baby boomers. In turn, the boomers may well be leaving at least some of that inherited wealth—along with the money they have earned in their lifetimes—to deserving nonprofit organizations like yours.

Let's take a look at some numbers. In 2010, MetLife commissioned a study, "Inheritance and Wealth Transfer to Baby Boomers," from Boston College's Center for Retirement Research. According to a December 27, 2010, article about the study on ABC News, "The study anticipates an inter-generational transfer of wealth totaling $11.6 trillion, including some $2.4 trillion that has already been gifted."

According to the US Trust report, "37 percent have never discussed legacy goals" and "44 percent have never discussed philanthropic strategy" with their financial advisors. That still leaves a majority—56 percent—who *have* had those discussions. And it's an exciting opportunity for those in the nonprofit sector to help educate those who haven't considered a philanthropic strategy or legacy goals.

Finally, an exciting trend in philanthropy has been emerging among billionaires—and the impact of this trend may well have the effect of encouraging "mere" millionaires to join in. The trend—really more of a movement, as you've probably heard—is called "The Giving Pledge." First made public by Warren Buffett and Bill Gates in 2010, the pledge commits billionaires to leaving at least half of their net worth to philanthropic causes when they die. As of a May 7, 2013, article in *CNN Money*, 114 billionaires had signed the pledge.

What Is Planned Giving?

Now that I've explained why you should have a plan for planned giving (so to speak), let's discuss what this type of gift is and how it works. Planned giving is any gift where the donor needs to do more than just write a check or pull out a charge card. (Think of it as the difference between buying that new outfit you saw on sale and deciding to buy a house.) In order to make a planned gift, donors consult with their financial and/or legal advisors and may choose to alter their wills, create trusts for your organization, designate your organization as the beneficiary of their life insurance, or donate real estate... There are many options for planned giving, both during the donor's life and after death. That said, roughly 90 percent of planned gifts are in the form of bequests—gifts made to your organization in a donor's will—and less than 10 percent are other, more complicated, types of gifts. Therefore, all you need to do to get started is accept bequests, and you'll be in the business of planned giving.

> Make it clear in all your materials and communications that you are not providing legal or financial advice to your donors, and encourage them to check with their own advisors before making planned gifts to your organization.
>
>

It's also important to note that the donor may not involve your organization in the decision to make a planned gift, so you'll want to treat all your donors as VIPs. However, the most likely people to leave your organization in their wills are your loyal, ongoing donors at any level. In other words, those donors who have given to your organization for ten years or more, regardless of the amount they regularly give.

Why Is It Important for Your Organization to Ask for Planned Gifts?

Just as the gifts you receive in a capital campaign are much larger than the ones you generally receive during your annual fund drive, planned gifts are often significantly larger than the donor would be willing or able to make with cash or a credit card. This is especially true in terms of bequests, because donors know they won't need the money they're leaving to you and, therefore, can afford to be more generous.

And since planned gifts are generally one-time gifts, as opposed to annual gifts—such as bequests, life insurance, real estate, etc.—they represent unique opportunities for your organization to do something special with the donation.

Contributions from planned gifts are also often the only (or best) way for organizations to start and grow endowments. As one-time gifts, bequests should not be used for your annual fund, because you won't be receiving the gift again next year. Therefore, it's best to designate bequest funding for long-term needs (unless the donor designates it for something specific) like an endowment-type fund.

As I mentioned above, your organization doesn't have to go to a huge amount of effort to ask for and receive planned gifts. You also don't need specially trained staff. Only hospitals and universities generally have the kinds of budgets that allow for specialized planned giving officers.

> You don't need any specialized skills or trained staff members to be able to accept planned gifts. Simply have an attorney and other strategic partners to call on as needed.
>
> What you *do* need to do is make it clear that your organization accepts planned gifts. This can be as simple as including standard text asking for bequests in your newsletter, on your website, and in your organization's other printed materials.
>
>

What Is an Endowment Fund?

An endowment fund is one where the organization invests the principal (initial donation) and then utilizes the interest (or a portion of the interest) for ongoing programs and services. Well-managed endowments can provide a reliable, stable source of income for your organization.

In other words, an endowment is a good thing to have, because the interest that is generated can be used to support the annual budget of your organization. That said, you will need a skilled and experienced investment committee and financial planner to oversee your organization's investments.

> An *endowment* is a donor-designated restricted fund where the principal is invested and not used by the organization. The interest generated by the fund is used for the operating budget.
>
> **definition**

There are several types of endowments including something called "quasi endowments," which are funds that act like endowments but are really board designated (as opposed to donor designated). The principal held in quasi-endowments can be used in certain circumstances, generally pending board approval.

If you have one or more financial professionals on your board you may choose to manage your endowment in-house. If not, there are several community foundations and other organizations that manage endowments for smaller nonprofits.

"You Want to Give Us What?" (the Importance of Strategic Partners in Planned Giving)

What would you do if a donor approached you about donating a charitable lead trust? Or if the donor wanted to set up a charitable gift annuity, gift of real estate, or life insurance policy?

Donors, particularly wealthier donors, like to make use of the tax advantages associated with different kinds of giving, and they may well approach you with an idea for a type of gift that you've never heard of.

Let's pretend a donor calls you offering to give your organization a piece of land in Florida. The donor wants to come by to bring you the deed tomorrow. You thank the donor, hang up, and excitedly tell your executive director the great news: Your organization is going to have some land to sell!

Two year later, you still have the land, which has turned out to be a swamp, or maybe even a Superfund cleanup site. It's going to cost your organization far more than the land is worth to sell it, even if you find a buyer. In the meantime, this "gift" continues to drain money from your operating funds.

To most people, any donation of land seems like a generous one, and most boards and staff members would be elated by that kind of gift. However, prudent organizations ask donors to sell the land and donate the proceeds, unless they have specific expertise in this area.

Your gifts policy should spell out in detail what your organization will do about any offers of gifts of land.

If (when) this happens, call upon your trusted advisors. Start with an attorney (hopefully you have at least one on your board) to point you in the right direction.

If you're approached by a donor who wants to make a gift you're unfamiliar with, be truthful and ask for details about just what the donor wants to do. Once you've gotten an explanation, let the donor know you need to confer with your advisors before proceeding.

Always recommend that donors consult their advisors before making planned gifts, and make it clear that you are unable to provide legal or financial advice of any kind.

Of course, before you even go to your advisor, consult your gifts policies to see whether your organization has determined it will accept this particular kind of gift.

Avoiding Trouble Before It Comes Up (Gifts Policies)

As I mentioned earlier, it's very important to have policies defining the types of planned gifts your organization will and will not accept. Such policies are simple to create and implement. In other words, don't wait until you're faced with an unusual planned gift to have a discussion about what to do!

Why are such policies important? Because they can save you from accepting a gift that will cost your organization more to receive than you will recoup by taking it—for example, gifts of land. Other kinds of planned gifts may be sufficiently complicated to administer that you and your board decide not to accept them as a matter of policy.

Land and complicated financial instruments aren't the only kinds of planned gifts for which you need to have defined policies. For example, several years ago when I was working full time as a development director, a donor called me and said she wanted to make a gift of artwork to my organization. What a generous idea! The problem, however, was that the organization I was working for wasn't a museum, nor was it in need of any art. With that in mind, I asked the donor if she would consider selling the art and donating the proceeds. Fortunately, she said yes. As it turned out, it would have cost us more to transport, store, and sell her gift than it turned out to be worth!

> ## Write Gift Acceptance Policies
>
> Meet with an ad hoc committee of your board (or your executive committee) to decide, and create a formal document describing, your organization's gift acceptance policies. Have the committee recommend these policies to the full board and vote on them. Once approved, create language for your newsletter, website, and other publications inviting donors to make planned gifts. If it's only bequests you're inviting donors to consider, that's fine.
>
>  to-do lists

While these samples will help guide your organization, keep in mind that they are not legal advice. Be sure to involve your board and/or legal and financial consultants when formalizing your own policy.

To Recap

◆ Planned gifts are simply gifts that take legal and financial planning on the part of the donor.

◆ Accepting planned gifts is easy—especially bequests, the most common type of planned gift.

◆ Donors are able to make larger gifts though planned gifts than they are when donating cash.

◆ Be sure your organization has a comprehensive gift acceptance policy.

Chapter Fifteen

Moving on Up: Taking Your Organization to the Next Level

IN THIS CHAPTER

···→ Moving your organization to the next stage of development

···→ Moving donors up the "donor pyramid"

···→ Donor retention versus donor acquisition

···→ Professional development: becoming a superstar major gifts fundraiser

My goal in writing this book is to help you become a better fundraiser, help your organization move to the next level of development and one step closer to achieving its mission, and show you how to help your donors become better philanthropists.

After all, your major gifts program isn't about the money you're going to raise—at least not in and of itself. Instead, your major gifts program is about what you're going to do with those funds: the children you'll feed, the animals you'll shelter, the disease you'll cure, the rain forest you're going to save from development.

That said, the point of this chapter is to give you a set of tools you can use to boost your success with starting and enhancing your major gifts program—and with all your fundraising work in the future.

Moving Your Organization to the Next Stage of Development

Just like individuals, nonprofit organizations have life cycles. However, nonprofits' life cycles aren't necessarily age dependent. I've worked with very old organizations that weren't very mature in terms of their development, and I've worked with new ones with development offices that were surprisingly mature.

Perhaps the most significant factor that determines whether a given organization will evolve and grow is whether or not that organization continually learns how to raise significantly more money—and to do so in new and different ways. For better or worse, progression means that the board and staff members are willing to take a risk and invest in development and growth. The good news is that these funds, in turn, allow you to do more and better work in your community.

Take a moment to think about how your own organization is doing in terms of your overall development. Here are some questions to ask yourself:

◆ Have you hired new staff members in the last year or two?

◆ Has your budget grown?

◆ Are you serving significantly more clients, or have you added new services?

◆ Have you moved to a larger location because you were in need of more space?

If you can answer yes to one or more of these questions, you know your organization is growing.

On the other hand, when I get a call from a thirty-year-old organization that has just one staff member—the executive director—I know I'm looking at a stagnant organization. (And, yes, I've had this happen many times!) It's often because the (founding) executive director and board members are in the mindset of "We do things this way because we've always done them this way." Sadly, they never have the opportunity to grow and serve more constituents.

If you can't answer yes to one or more of the questions I've posed above, it's time to take some time to evaluate what needs to be accomplished to allow your nonprofit to start growing again. You may need to focus your attention on your development office alone. Or, if your organization has been stagnant for some time, you may need to look at the overall state of your nonprofit, including the programmatic side, the board members, and the staff. Are you having trouble raising more money from new

---

I was recently hired by a homeless shelter to consult with it about its board. The majority of the board members had been serving for ten years or more, and while the bylaws had term limits in them, they weren't being enforced. In addition, there were no set terms for officers; therefore, the same members had been on the executive committee for more than five years. It was time to overhaul the board by bringing in new talent, new ideas, new skill sets, and individuals with new connections and networks.

While the changes didn't occur overnight, after two years, the board had an entirely new makeup—and the new, energized board went on to make some bold decisions that resulted in significant growth and development for the shelter, including new residences, programs, services, and the ability to serve significantly more people in meaningful ways.

Is your board holding your organization back?

stories from
the real world

sources because you need to do something different as a fundraising office—or because your programs need to be updated to be more useful to your community and be more relevant and exciting to prospective donors? Does your board need an overhaul? Do you need a change of staff?

You may even need to ask yourself whether or not your organization has served its purpose. Is it time to close up shop, or is it time to recommit to your original mission while finding new ways to serve that mission?

Obviously, this isn't a set of questions for you to tackle alone, even if the issues you're facing need to be addressed at "just" the fundraising level. If your organization has become stagnant, it's time to bring together your entire senior staff and board to figure out exactly how you've gotten to this place—and what you are willing and able to do to get out of it.

After all, growth requires a willingness to take risks and make mistakes. In addition to stepping into the realm of major gifts, and (probably) other fundraising ventures, growing means challenging your organization on the programmatic side as well. You may well need to add staff, recruit new board members, or maybe even let some existing board members or staff move on to other things. There's also a chance you'll lose some donors who like things just the way they are, even as you attract new donors who are inspired by your new energy.

◆ Schedule an internal meeting to discuss growth at your organization with key staff members. If you are a staff of only one or two people, invite key board members to discuss a strategy for growth. Do you have an updated strategic plan? Are you following it?

◆ If you don't already have one, create a strategic plan for the next three to five years. If you are serious about growth, invest in a strategic planning consultant to help you through the process. Ask board members to make a special donation to help cover the consultant's cost. This financial commitment will demonstrate whether or not they are invested (literally and figuratively) in your growth potential.

◆ Evaluate whether or not there is additional need for your programs and services. Are you currently meeting the need, or does additional need exist? Are there competing organizations meeting the need? Will the need continue into the foreseeable future?

to-do lists

Taking the leap to the next level (whatever that will mean for your organization) is an exhilarating, stressful, energizing, and sometimes frustrating process. Most of all, it's a process that requires commitment.

Are your board and staff finally ready to make that leap? If not, what do you need to do to get ready?

Moving Donors Up the "Donor Pyramid"

Have you heard the term "donor pyramid"? You may also have heard this concept referred to as the "donor ladder." These are the terms the fundraising world uses to describe the process of getting donors to give larger gifts over time. When we talk about the donor pyramid, we're talking about moving donors up from smaller annual gifts to major gifts to your annual fund—and positioning them to give ever larger gifts to your future capital campaign and, eventually, to make a planned gifts (see pyramid below).

To grow your annual fund, it's necessary not only to recruit ever more donors but, more importantly, to also inspire each of your donors to give increasingly more money over time. To do this, you need to ask for increasing amounts—not every single year, but over a period of years. This, by the way, is one of the many reasons it's important to ask for a specific amount, whether you're asking for an annual fund gift in a letter or a major gift in person. This is also why an up-to-date and accurate donor database (which we discussed earlier) is an absolutely essential tool.

The concept of the donor pyramid acknowledges a few important realities about donors and stewardship. For one thing, ability to give changes over time as a donor's career changes and matures. If the person who gave you twenty-five dollars a year as an administrative assistant is still giving you twenty-five dollars a year as a CEO many years later, you're doing something wrong!

> The *donor pyramid* (or donor ladder) refers to the process of successfully encouraging donors to give larger amounts over time.
>
> **de**finition

In addition, the donor pyramid is also part of your stewardship process. Obviously you're going to spend more resources cultivating donors who are already making major gifts than you do on your twenty-five-dollar donors. That said, though, you will still be doing at least some cultivation with everyone who gives. And those efforts, along your organization's great work, will pay off over time.

Here's an example of what the steps in a typical donor pyramid might look like (let's call our hypothetical donor "Joe"):

1. Year one: For his first gift, Joe donates $25.

2. Year two: Joe chooses to give again—and, again, he gives $25.

3. Year three: This year, you ask for $50 and Joe gives $35.

4. Year four: You ask for $50; Joe gives $50.

5. Year five: You ask for $50; Joe gives $50.

Notice that you're not asking for more money each year. Instead, you're asking Joe to give the same amount for a few years before asking him to increase his gift again. Why? Because by waiting, you're giving Joe a chance to continually learn more about your organization, become increasingly committed to your cause—and, depending on how old (and thus how new in his career) Joe is when he starts making gifts, you're also giving him a chance to increase his income and with it his capacity to give.

6. Year six: This year, you ask for $150, and Joe gives $150.

Congratulations! You're moving Joe up the giving pyramid! Steward Joe properly, and he is likely to continue to increase his gifts as his income increases. In time—and, of course, depending on his circumstances—Joe may well join the leagues of your major annual gift or even your capital campaign donors. And even if he is unable to reach those heights, he may well remember your organization generously in his will.

If you're not asking for specific amounts of money, your donors are likely to continue to give the same amount every year. Help ensure you are moving their giving up by asking for increasingly larger amounts of money over time. Increases may be small at first—like from $25 to $50, but eventually, as they become more engaged and committed to your organization, you may see a jump to $500, $1,000, or more.

Here is an example of a giving pyramid. Your goal is to try to get some donors to increase their annual giving to the point of giving major gifts. A few of these donors (as well as a few who haven't been able to make major gifts) will ultimately make planned gifts as well.

One reason it's in a pyramid shape is that the fewest donors make it to the top of the pyramid, and the majority of your donors are at the base.

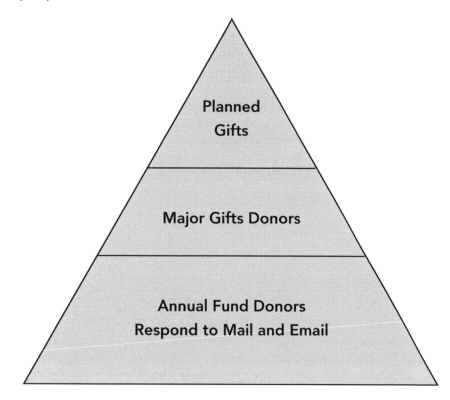

A final note on the donor pyramid: It's important to remember that not all of your donors will reach the major giving heights. In fact, most of them won't. If you remember earlier in the book, we talked about the fact that 10 percent of your donors will always end up giving 90 percent of the gifts.

So why have a donor pyramid at all? For one thing, because you'll never know who is willing and able to reach the top until you try to get them there. And for another, think about your progress with our hypothetical donor, Joe. If you had never asked Joe for first fifty dollars and then one hundred dollars, there's a very good chance he would have kept giving twenty-five dollars every year. Even if Joe is never able to make a major gift or help with a capital campaign, which would you rather have? Joe's original twenty-five dollars a year or incrementally larger gifts over the course of many years?

> The donor pyramid won't ensure that every one of your donors will become a major gift givers. What it will do, however—if you steward your donors correctly—is make sure that several of your donors are giving as much as they're able to give and/or increasing the amounts they give over time.
>
>

Donor Retention and Attrition

In addition to how much your donors give each year, it's also important to understand and pay attention to the rates of donor retention and attrition at your organization. Acquiring new donors is significantly more expensive than soliciting repeat or loyal donors.

To use just one measurement, let's look at the cost to acquire a new donor via direct mail versus the cost to renew a donor in the same manner. According to a December 2013 report on the website supportingadvancement.com, it costs an average of twenty cents per dollar raised to renew donors via direct mail.

Would you like to try to guess how much it costs to acquire a new donor via the same method? It costs between $1.00 and $1.25 per dollar raised—in other words, at least five times more! (Of course, after you acquire and keep a new donor, the initial cost pays off, but it often takes several years to realize the financial benefit of donor acquisition.)

Not only that, but new donors generally give less than repeat donors who have gotten to know your organization and thus increased their gifts over time.

Finally, remember the donor pyramid? Believe me, it's much easier (and faster) to move a donor from the middle of that pyramid to the top than it is to move a donor from the bottom level to the top level.

For these reasons, I recommend running a report on your donor retention rates every year—not just your major donors, but all of your individual donors—and comparing your results for the past three to five years so you can spot any emerging trends.

If you find that your donor retention rate is going up, congratulations! Try to figure out exactly what you're doing to make that happen and see how you can refine your donor cultivation process to do even better!

On the other hand, if you're seeing decreasing retention rates, it's time to do some serious evaluation. First, look at your overall cultivation process. Are you thanking donors in a timely manner? Do you stay in touch with them through the year as appropriate? Do you tell them how their gifts are being used? As I discussed earlier, proper donor cultivation is one of the main keys to fundraising success—and not just with major gifts, but with donor retention as well.

If your cultivation process seems up to speed, you may need to broaden your evaluation to look at factors such as your area's local economy and how organizations similar to your own are doing with retention.

Finally, of course, take a look at your programs and the effectiveness of your organization overall. This is another topic I've discussed before, but it bears repeating. Are you still fulfilling a vital mission in your community, or does your organization need to change focus, change programs, or perhaps even look into merging with another local organization that's focusing on the same areas?

Despite everything I've said above, don't start thinking I want you to stop working on acquiring new donors. Far from it! After all, life happens. Even the most loyal donors move, suffer through events like job losses or deaths in the family, and even pass away themselves. Even if your organization were to maintain a near-miraculous donor retention rate of 100 percent for, say, two years, you could safely bet a year's salary that your good fortune will not last.

So, yes, pay close attention to—and spend most of your efforts on—donor retention. In addition, though, always be on the lookout for ways to recruit the new donors today who will become your loyal donors in the months and years to come.

Professional Development: Becoming a Superstar Major Gifts Fundraiser

The concept of professional development is a relatively new thing in the fundraising field. For example, our leading professional organization, the Association of Fundraising Professionals (AFP), has existed since only 1960.

When it comes to professional training, the facts are even more startling. Indiana University's School of Philanthropy was the first academic program to offer degree programs in our field— and it wasn't founded until 1987! That's right—fundraising has been recognized as a profession worthy of advanced-level academic preparation for roughly less than thirty years.

Increasingly, people who are newly entering the field of fundraising, particularly at the higher levels, have received at least some professional training. But the fact remains that many, if not most, fundraisers today didn't begin their careers in the classroom but instead have had to rely entirely on more experienced mentors, books (and, today, websites), and on-the-job training.

As a small-shop development professional, there's a very good chance that you don't have either the time or the funds to study for an advanced degree in fundraising while also working what (for most of us) is well over a forty-hour week. That doesn't mean, however, that professional development is out of your reach!

Here are a few of the things that you can do to become a superstar major gifts (and overall) fundraiser:

◆ Find a mentor. Most people who go into nonprofit work do so because we love to give to others, and fundraising professionals are no exception. If there's no one in your office who is more experienced than you are—and the chances of that are pretty high in most small shops—take some time to network and find the experienced fundraisers who work in your community. Chances are that one or more of them will be happy to provide you occasional advice, and one may become a fantastic professional mentor.

◆ Join the Association of Fundraising Professionals—and get involved. I have to admit to some bias on this point, as I am currently the president of the New Jersey chapter of AFP. That said, the reason I'm so involved with this organization is because together we are setting high standards for our field and providing the training and programming to allow fundraisers to pursue professional development opportunities without having the time and expense of obtaining a formal degree. I also credit AFP with providing me all of my early, formal fundraising training, which is why became involved in the first place—and stay involved!

◆ Attend at least one professional conference a year. Whether you choose an AFP conference or another event, give yourself and your organization the gift of a few days during which you turn off your phone, walk away from your email, and soak up the latest developments in our field. Conferences are also great places to find professional mentors!

◆ Subscribe to and read fundraising-related online and off-line publications. Even if you can spend only fifteen minutes or so a week on this activity, I promise you will come away with ideas that will help you further excel in your work. You can even start with my blog. It's on my website at tripointfundraising.com/fundraising-tips, and it's free!

◆ Try something new. I included this idea in my blog as part of a post about ways to make fundraising fun again, but it's equally important from the perspective of professional development. If you've never tried a social media campaign, take the plunge. If you've been using the same messaging in your annual holiday mailing, try changing everything up—from the formatting to the tone of the mailing this year. Trying new things—and doing the activities you've done before in new and different ways—is a great method to both spice up your day and discover great new ways to raise more money! However, before going full force, I recommend testing your new strategy with a segment of your list. But if you stick to the methods you've always used, you will continue to get what you've always gotten!

◆ Get out and talk to your donors—and don't ask them for money. This is another tip from my blog post on making fundraising fun—and another one that can lead to a great professional development experience. Meet a few select donors in their homes or offices to ask them about themselves—and about the job they feel you and your office are doing. Why were they attracted to your nonprofit the first time? Why do they give? Do they have any ideas about ways you could make their experience as donors even better? Of course, this is a big part of cultivation, and you should be doing this as part of your new raising major gifts effort anyway.

◆ Take a class. I'm a big advocate of continuing education. If a degree is beyond your reach, take a class—either online or in person—to help you take your effectiveness to a whole new level.

As you may have guessed from the chapter of this book about online giving alone, ours is a rapidly changing and expanding field. It's also a field that's becoming increasingly specialized, particularly in terms of developing technologies. These days, professional development isn't just a *plus*—it's a *must* for every fundraiser who wants to make significant contributions to the nonprofits they serve.

To Recap

◆ Ensure your organization and development efforts are growing by doing a quick analysis of how your organization is doing overall.

◆ Move donors up the donor pyramid by asking for increasingly larger gifts over time.

◆ Donor retention is hugely important for several reasons. Every year, be sure to run a report to determine how well you're doing in this area—and take the time to make the necessary changes to improve your progress.

◆ Ensure you are growing professionally by attending conferences, classes, or trainings each year.

Appendix

Finding Five Hours a Week

Throughout the majority of this book, I've been telling you that you can increase your organization's bottom line by putting just five hours a week toward major gift fundraising.

I've given you the step-by-step process to make this happen. We've talked about preparing your board, creating and maintaining your database, identifying prospects, the important art of cultivation, and the solicitation (or ask) and stewardship of those donors.

However, there is one very important question that may still be on your mind:

"This is all wonderful, but how am I supposed to find five hours a week?"

I'm well aware that very few small shop development professionals stop at forty hours' work each week. Most people reading this book are probably working more like forty-five to fifty, and maybe even sixty, hours a week already. With that in mind, the last thing I want you to do is to add another five hours to your already-overbooked schedule!

Instead, I want you to carve out just five hours a week from your existing schedule and to use that time to create the major gifts program that will help your organization grow—and enable you to hire some help!

The purpose of this section isn't to talk about time management overall. You can find hundreds of books, blog posts, articles, etc., that will help you manage your time in sixty-, thirty-, and even five-minute intervals!

Instead, I'd like to concentrate on four steps you can start to take right now to create the time you need to make major gifts happen: recruit support, delegate, evaluate, and guard.

1. *Recruit support.* Early in the book, I discussed getting your board and executive director involved in the major gifts process. But while their involvement is vital to your success with major gifts, it doesn't end with giving and getting. They also need to understand that you need their support in other ways as well, including their support for you taking the time necessary to begin your major gifts program.

2. *Delegate.* This is related to recruiting support, because once you have your board on board (so to speak) with your major gifts program, it's time to ask for help. Perhaps one of your members owns or is a partner in a firm that has substantial administrative support. Could that member donate some admin staff member help with data entry or scheduling meetings?

   Delegation isn't restricted to your board. Do you have volunteers who can be trained to input data in your database, welcome visitors, or even make the coffee? Any task that can be taken off your plate should be so that you have the time and focus for major gifts (as well as your other responsibilities).

3. *Evaluate.* In the **Introduction**, I mentioned that you may have to give something up in order to carve out the five hours a week you need to be putting toward major gifts. That's what this stage is about. Is there anything you're currently spending time on that doesn't have a significant return on investment—for example, an event that may be popular, but doesn't actually raise much (if any) funding? If so, this might be the time to either employ delegation—ask board members and/or volunteers to create a committee to make this event or other activity happen—or put it on hold so you can concentrate on major gifts.

4. *Guard.* As in guard your time. Each week, make sure you've marked the time you'll be spending on major gifts the next week with a big red "do not disturb" *X* and that your board and other staff know that this time is devoted to major gifts—and only major gifts. If possible, in fact, set that time aside for the next year right now and plan for the tasks you may have to delegate to make those hours happen. If you've persuaded your board and executive director to pursue major gifts, they should be happy to see you making this program a priority!

And remember, the five hours per week can be used as needed. It could mean five hours in one day per week or one hour every day. It's up to you, and it will likely change depending on the task and your other activities.

The most important thing to remember is that you will need to spend time and effort in order to raise major gifts. It doesn't happen overnight, but you can do it! Stick with it for one year, and if you devote five hours per week, every week, I promise you will raise significantly more money this year.

Calendar—Five Hours per Week (Sample)

Month	Week One	Week Two	Week Three	Week Four
January	Run reports to identify prospects	Meet with committee to narrow list	Plan board retreat	
February	Research prospects		Create cultivation plans for top twenty	Development committee meeting
March	Hold board retreat	Send personalized notes to prospects		
April	Give tours to prospects		Give tours to prospects	Development committee meeting
May	Meet and greet at gala	Face-to-face meetings with two prospects	Follow up on prospect meetings	Face-to-face meetings with two prospects
June	Follow up on prospect meetings		Face-to-face meetings with two prospects	Follow up on prospect meetings
July	Face-to-face meetings with two prospects	Follow up on prospect meetings		Development committee meeting
August	More cultivation activities			
September	Send program update	Prepare volunteers for solicitation	Prepare volunteers for solicitation	Development committee meeting
October	Two solicitation meetings	Follow up from meetings	Two solicitation meetings	Follow-up from meetings
November	Two solicitation meetings	Follow up from meetings	Two solicitation meetings	Development committee meeting
December	Send handwritten holiday cards	Send handwritten holiday cards	Follow-up calls	

Note: This is just an example. Your five hours per week will not be this neat and tidy, but it may be a combination of activities. I wish I could give you an exact calendar, but it will be different for everyone—depending on you and your organization. However, you can use this type of chart to plan your time.

Calendar—Five Hours per Week

Use this calendar to plan your five hours per week. Some tasks will take more than five hours and will stretch over multiple weeks or months, like cultivation. Other tasks will take less than five hours. Each week and month will be different, depending on where you are in the process with each individual prospect. It is unlikely that you will be able to complete this table in advance. Try to plan out at least four weeks in advance with each of your tasks.

Month	Week One	Week Two	Week Three	Week Four
January				
February				
March				
April				
May				
June				
July				
August				
September				
October				
November				
December				

Index

If you enjoyed this book, you'll want to pick up the other books in the CharityChannel Press **In the Trenches**™ series.

CharityChannel.com/bookstore

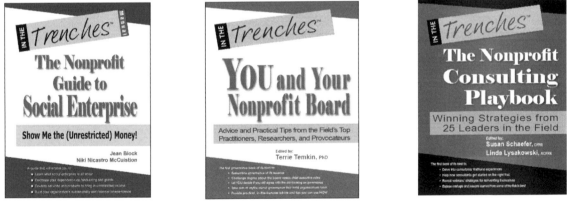

In addition, there are dozens of titles currently moving to publication.
So be sure to check the CharityChannel.com bookstore.

CharityChannel.com/bookstore

Fundraising
Second Edition

for the GENIUS ™

A complete course in nonprofit fundraising

Linda Lysakowski

FOR THE GENIUS IN ALL OF US ™

ForTheGENIUS.com/bookstore

for the GENIUS
PRESS

Caregiving

for the GENIUS™

Understand the Journey
from the Inside Out

Jane W. Barton

FOR THE GENIUS IN ALL OF US™

ForTheGENIUS.com/bookstore

for the GENIUS™

PRESS

ForTheGENIUS.com/bookstore

PRESS

Made in the USA
San Bernardino, CA
07 May 2014